The Insubordination of Signs

POST-CONTEMPORARY INTERVENTIONS

Series Editors: Stanley Fish and Fredric Jameson

LATIN AMERICA IN TRANSLATION/

EN TRADUCCIÓN/EM TRADUÇÃO

The Insubordination of Signs

Political Change, Cultural Transformation,

and Poetics of the Crisis

NELLY RICHARD

Alice A. Nelson and Silvia R. Tandeciarz, Translators

DUKE UNIVERSITY PRESS Durham & London 2004

In memory of Germán Bravo, for those moments

when what he called a "gentle inquiry into the insuturable

character of questions of meaning" fails.

Contents

Author's Note

This edition brings together five texts that converge on a single problematic: the interplay of tensions between culture and society, aesthetics and politics, signs and ideologies. The stage on which these tensions are debated corresponds to Chile in the 1980s and early 1990s. The book analyzes the meaning of the discursive strategies constructed by the political culture of the left, the aesthetic neo–avant-garde, and the alternative movement in the social sciences, including their problematic differences. But the questions contained in this analysis go beyond their contextual referent to engage in a discussion—vital for any cultural and political context—regarding the relationships between institutional discourses and critiques of representation, constituted and informal forms of knowledge, social identity and subjectivity in crisis, legitimized practices and those situated at the margins of organized cultural systems.

Other than "Roturas, memoria y descontinuidades (homenaje a W. Benjamin)" [Ruptures, Memory, and Discontinuities (Homage to Walter Benjamin)], the chapters are revised and transformed versions of previous publications and talks. Chapter 2 first appeared as "Una cita limítrofe entre neovanguardia y postvanguardia" [A Border Citation: Between Neo– and Post–Avant-Garde] in the anthology *Modernidade: Vanguardias artísticas na América Latina* [Modernity: Artistic Avant-Gardes in Latin America] (Sao Paulo: Memorial/Unesp, 1990). Chapter 3, "Destrucción/reconstrucción/desconstrucción" [Destruction, Reconstruction, and Deconstruction], was published in the journal *Nueva sociedad* (Caracas) 116 (November/December 1991). Chapter 4, "En torno a las ciencias sociales: Líneas de fuerza y puntos de fuga" [The Social Sciences: Front Lines and Points of Retreat], is based on a paper delivered at the first meeting of the Inter-American Cultural Studies Network, organized by the Center for Social Research, City University of New York, and the Universidad Autónoma Metropolitana [UNAM], which took place in Mexico City in May 1993. Chapter 5, "Escenario democrático y política de las diferencias" [Staging Democracy and the Politics of Difference], was published in the *Revista de crítica cultural* (Santiago) 5 (June 1992).

Translators' Acknowledgments

We relied upon the expertise of many individuals in the completion of this translation, and to them we would like to extend our sincere gratitude. Kathleen Ross, John French, Juan Poblete, Alberto Moreiras, Patrick Hub, and Pablo Yáñez all offered valuable feedback and encouragement at critical points in the process. Bill Arney, Susan Fiksdal, Alan Nasser, and David Marr helped us capture a few key terms more exactly in English. The superb editorial work of J. Reynolds Smith, Sharon P. Torian, and Kate Lothman strengthened the manuscript, and their patience through several unfortunate delays helped us bring the project to fruition. Our home institutions, the College of William and Mary and the Evergreen State College, gave us crucial research support and facilities to complete the project. And, without the support of our families — Pablo, Ximena, Cristóbal, Patrick — none of this would have been possible. Finally, we are grateful for the trust Nelly Richard placed in us; we hope our rendering of her work into English will help to convey our deepest appreciation.

Translators' Preface

Nelly Richard figures among the most prominent cultural critics writing in Latin America today. As part of the Chilean neo–avant-garde that emerged during the Pinochet dictatorship (1973–90), Richard worked to expand and deepen the possibilities for cultural debate within that constrained context and has continued to offer incisive cultural commentary about the country's transition to democracy. Richard's rigorous essays and books engage questions of Latin American identity within the context of North/South debates on postmodernism and neoliberalism, with a strong emphasis on gender analysis and micropolitical strategies of resistance. Well known as the founder and director of the influential *Revista de crítica cultural* (Santiago, Chile), Richard has been central to the dissemination throughout Latin America of work by key contemporary thinkers, including Beatriz Sarlo, Néstor García Canclini, Jacques Derrida, Ernesto Laclau, Fredric Jameson, Jesús Martín Barbero, and Diamela Eltit. Like Richard's own essays, the *Revista* has put into dialogue theoretical perspectives from Latin America, Europe, and the United States, creating a lively forum for intellectual debate on culture, theory, and politics since its founding in 1990.[1]

Born in France, Richard completed her degree in literature at the Sorbonne and moved to Chile in 1970, a year characterized by the euphoric victory of Unidad Popular (Popular Unity) under the leadership of the democratically elected socialist president Salvador Allende. During the Popular Unity period, Richard served as coordinator of art exhibitions for the Museo de Bellas Artes in Santiago, a post that she abandoned after the violent overthrow of Allende in 1973. Under the Pinochet dictatorship, Richard became involved with unofficial art circuits, aligning herself within the margins of opposition to the military regime, as both a protagonist and an analyst of the neo–avant-garde (or *avanzada*) cultural scene. The essays in this book bear traces of that time, whether in Richard's emphasis on alternative artists and art movements, such as CADA (*Colectivo de Acciones de Arte* [Art Actions Collective]), or in her piecing together fragments of art history and criticism first circulated precariously as photocopies under the military regime.

Richard was also closely connected to the feminist movement reconstituted slowly in various pockets throughout the country. Although many of those engaged in oppositional activities from the beginning of the Pinochet years were women, a feminist movement only received public acknowledgment as such after the eruption of massive national protests in 1983–84. As Julieta Kirkwood and other Chilean feminists noted, the ways in which power operated under the military regime had made feminist analysis not only particularly relevant but also politically necessary. In 1987, Richard served as one of the main organizers of what would prove to be the most significant literary event under the dictatorship — indeed, one of the most important in all of Latin America during the 1980s — the Primer Congreso de Literatura Femenina Latinoamericana (First International Conference on Latin American Women's Literature), held in Santiago in August of that year. As is evident in *Escribir en los bordes*, a published collection of essays from the conference, this gathering raised questions of difference and institutional exclusions faced by women writers and resituated debates on *écriture féminine* within particularly Latin American cultural coordinates. Richard's *Masculino/femenino*, published in 1993, revisits key questions from this conference, reconsidering them in light of Chile's return to democracy.

Like *Masculino/femenino*, Richard's other collections — particularly *La estratificación de los márgenes* (1989), *La insubordinación de los signos* (1994), and *Residuos y metáforas* (1998) — have insisted on micropractices of difference and an aesthetic of the fragmentary, partial, and oblique as opening new discursive and artistic possibilities for contesting hegemonic discourses. Her own challenging, suggestive prose style underscores this stance and resonates with the neo-avant-garde impulse of writers like Diamela Eltit. Situated at the intersections of literary criticism, art history, aesthetics, philosophy, and feminist theory, Richard's work seeks to illuminate the complex relationships between institutional and contestatory discourses, between legitimized and marginalized practices, and between established social identities and subjectivities in crisis. And, far from seeing her work as completed with democracy's return, she has insisted that the consensus-driven Chilean transition has necessitated a renewed commitment to debate. As Richard writes in *Residuos y metáforas*: "I think it is necessary to defend the secret of these opacities and refractions against the linguistic tyranny of the simple, direct, and transparent discourse characterizing today's social communications, which have left language without narrative twists, without poetic turns of double and ambiguous meanings."[2] In the context of the Chilean democracy's suppressed contradictions, Richard contends that cultural criticism should "make readers suspicious of the false assumption that forms are innocent and languages transparent, an assumption hiding the fact that pacts and agreements of shared interests tacitly restrain [other] values, meanings, and forms of power."[3] Critical writing, she asserts, should inspire readers to "break the mold of prefabricated meaning."[4]

Clearly interdisciplinary, Richard's critical practice is distinguished by her sustained focus on the margins, borders, and interstices of cultural expression as those sites illuminating the most salient social conflicts—questions of power and exclusion—and bearing traces of desire, including those for social change. While one could subsume her work under the label of *cultural studies*, she herself designates it *cultural criticism* or *cultural critique*, a distinction that has garnered its own academic following, both through Richard's seminars at the alternative university ARCIS in Santiago and through the *Revista de crítica cultural*. As Ana del Sarto explains it, "Cultural Critique construes its locus from aesthetic materiality, in order to 'critically transform the real' . . . while Cultural Studies construes it from social materiality, in order critically to produce social reality."[5] While the differences between these two forms of cultural practice have led to healthy philosophical debates, what we would like to stress here is not so much the usefulness or validity of one over the other, but rather Richard's own sense of alterity vis-à-vis dominant discourses and the historical conditions in which her work is embedded.[6]

Taken as a body of work, then, Richard's essays have proven instrumental in reclaiming so-called high art (or avant-garde aesthetic practices) for a progressive political project of institutional, cultural, economic, and social critique—a claim particularly significant in the face of the traditional left's historical rejection of such aesthetically oriented practices as complicit with bourgeois or statist interests. In this regard, Richard's work resonates strongly in a U.S. academic context shaken by the advent of cultural studies, a context marked by struggles to reconcile old disciplinary perspectives emphasizing aesthetics with interdisciplinary approaches to culture broadly defined as the practice of everyday life. Paradoxically positioned between tradition and innovation, Richard is one of the few contemporary critics to successfully bridge literary criticism and aesthetic critique, visual arts and narrative, social practices and representation.

While Richard's practice emerged in a specific local register and insistently positions itself within the Chilean and Latin American contexts, we are convinced that through a sustained commitment to translation, her local observations will have a decisive impact on the global cultural field.[7] We hope that "this analysis, as its bond to another culture is rendered more explicit, will only be assisted in leading readers to uncover for themselves, in their own situation, their own tactics, their own creations, and their own initiatives."[8] We hope that our renderings of Nelly Richard's essays not only conserve the rigor of her prose but also stimulate English-speaking readers to accept her challenge to engage meaningfully in their own cultural critiques.

Note on This Translation

Throughout the text, words in quotation marks or italics follow the author's usage in the original Spanish. In a few instances, we have included terms from the Spanish-language original, italicized and in brackets after our English translation, in order to convey further nuance for readers of Spanish.

Richard quotes from a range of sources, mostly in the Spanish original or in Spanish translation. When these quotes were available in English translation, we used the standard published version and referenced them in the bibliography in place of the Spanish. When translations were not available, we translated the extracts ourselves. The bibliography contains only those sources cited by Richard herself, and not those referenced by the translators in the preface and notes. Likewise, in order to conserve Richard's original endnote numbers, translators' notes are indicated by typographic symbols rather than numbers in the text.

In some cases, bibliographic citations in the original text were incomplete; we have remedied this whenever possible. For information on the sources originally quoted by the author, please refer to the Spanish-language edition of this work.

ONE

Ruptures, Memory, and Discontinuities
(Homage to Walter Benjamin)

REINVENTING MEMORY

Within the entire symbolic repertoire of the last two decades of
Chilean history,* the figure of memory has been most strongly dramatized by the unresolved tension between *recollection* and *forgetting*
(between latency and death, revelation and concealment, proof and
denial, theft and restitution). The subject of human rights abuses
has sharply marked all Chilean narrative about the national body
with images of human remains: of bodies that have not been found,
bodies that have not been laid to rest. This lack of burial is the image
—*without recovery*—of a historical mourning process, one that never
completely assimilates the sense of loss, but rather conserves it in an
unfinished, transitional version.[1] It is also the metaphorical condition of an *unsealed* temporality: inconclusive, and therefore open to
reexploration in many new directions by our memory, increasingly
active and dissatisfied.

In the dismembered landscape of postcoup Chile, three issues
have caused memory, compulsively, to provoke ruptures, links, and
discontinuities. First, the threat of its *loss*, when those taking power
in 1973 partitioned and mutilated the past prior to the military regime's foundational break. Second, the task of its *recuperation*, when
the country started to recover the social ties recomposing its democratic tradition. And, third, the official challenge of its *pacification*,
when today, a community divided by the trauma of homicidal violence must be reunited on the postdictatorial stage, suturing the
edges of a wound that separates punishment from forgiveness.

But the recent history of Chilean memory should not be summed up as a linear and progressive sequence of gestures harmoniously converging toward one and the same result: that of returning *one* meaning ("its" unique and true meaning) to a national-historical corpus disintegrated by breaks with tradition. Semi-obscured in a plot that subsumes the more residual history of these breaks lie hidden the still clandestine threads of many other artistic and cultural memories, memories that rebelled against the ideological determinism of rationalities unified by final and totalizing truths. If we are to extract a lesson from the relearning of memory that bodies and languages had to practice in the Chile of forgetfulness [*de la desmemoria*, "disremembering"], it is knowing that the past is not a time irreversibly seized and frozen in recollection under the rubric of what *already was*, thus condemning memory to follow the dictum of obediently reestablishing its own continuity. Instead, the past is a field of citations, crisscrossed as much by continuity (the various forms of supposing or imposing an idea of succession) as by discontinuity (by cuts that interrupt the dependence of that succession on a predetermined chronology). It simply takes certain critical junctures to unleash that heterodox reformulation, for memories bound by history to undo the knots of their discordant temporalities.

The dramatization of memory is played out today in the context of political contingency, but it was also played out in those Chilean cultural works that, during the dictatorship, committed dispossession to memory using an alphabet of survival.† This was an alphabet of marks to be recycled via the precarious economies of the fragmentary and of the trace [*del trozo y de la traza*].

Those works elaborated various techniques for reinventing memory in the shadow of a history full of violent forced entries and oppositional struggle. In almost all of them, and not by mere coincidence, resounds the echo of significations derived from the drift of Benjaminian influence. It is not that such works were responding directly to Walter Benjamin's texts, following correspondences prearranged by erudite bibliographical transfers. Benjamin was never part of the corpus of theoretical references handled within Chilean universities by literary critics on the left, who could have welcomed him in: "[The characteristics of Benjamin's work]—his atypical Marxism, more like scaffolding than a central plot, the distance in his thought from globalizing constructions and ideological alignments, his disposition toward the insertion of cultural residues, layers of meaning hidden in the corners or margins of texts—were not perhaps the most pertinent for a criticism that needed to address a social and political emergency that required less oblique forms of analysis."[2] But this does not mean that Benjamin's thought has not become a real force for critical intervention in the Chilean cultural milieu. Instead, it means that the productivity of that force unfolded outside the university's walls, and that it was not channeled via a preconstituted lesson, but rather flowed dispersedly and heterogeneously, as Benjamin himself had proposed: "What is decisive is not the progression from one piece of knowledge to the next, but the leap implicit in any one piece of knowledge. This is the inconspicuous mark of authenticity which distinguishes it from every kind of standard product that has been mass produced."[3]

Chilean works colluded with Walter Benjamin's texts, forgoing in many instances the theoretical contours of knowledge produced within the university and weaving through his chiaroscuros without needing to recur to the academic mediation of a formally designed line of thought. Instead, these works were inspired by a certain kinship that secretly aligned them, without premeditated agendas or methods. A mixture of chance and necessity wound up making several Benjaminian references productive, through "the combinations, permutations, [and] utilizations" of concepts whose pertinence and validity "are never interior, but rather depend on their interconnectedness with one or another exterior,"[4] as Deleuze and Guattari signaled in their defense of the *experimentality* of meaning.

Beyond trying to discover conceptual or theoretical filiations owed to some matrix of knowledge, it seems more worthwhile to allow ourselves to be surprised by the itinerary of semidisconnected references that etched Benjamin into the Chilean histories of memory and its erasures. And it also seems worthwhile to ask: "Why does

Benjamin return, that Berliner from between the World Wars, on a train to an empty station, to descend upon a foggy platform so close to us?"[5]

What follows is an attempt to gather some of the disparate threads that weave together a Benjaminian reading of the interrupted and assailed memories of some cultural practices within our recent history.

STRATEGIES OF THE REFRACTORY

The first Chilean hypothesis of a "refractory art" to emerge during the dictatorship intersected with a recollection of Benjamin's will to forge "concepts which . . . [would be] completely useless for the purposes of Fascism."[6] This art was "refractory" in both senses of the word: as a "tenacious negation" and as a "deviation from a route that preceded it."[7] Referring to this first stage of artistic production after the coup (and taking as examples works by Enrique Lihn, Raúl Zurita, Eugenio Dittborn, Roser Bru, etc.), Adriana Valdés pointed out how certain works "were produced in order to be unassimilable by any 'official' cultural system." They were works that proposed something that a totalitarian logic would find impossible to take advantage of or appropriate, something useless for fitting "in the system of exchange, in the economy, [or] in circulation within that system, not even as an explicit sign of dissidence."[8]

To have formulated meanings that were merely contrary to the dominant point of view, without taking aim at the larger order of its signifying structures, would have meant remaining inscribed within the same linear duality of a Manichaean construction of meaning. It would have meant inverting the symmetry of what was represented, without questioning the topology of the representation. It is true that the predominant tendency of Chilean contestatory art utilized by the traditional left sought above all to take revenge on the dictatorial offense by plotting—in its symmetrical inverse—an epic of resistance that would be the photographic negative of the official "take." But, on the flanks of that heroic and monumental art, new creative works battled—works that refused to attend to the merely figurative con-tingency of the "NO," without simultaneously critiquing the entire discursive regime responsible for transforming the dogmatic rigidity of "YES" versus "NO" into an imprisoning paradigm.‡

The boundary to establish and defend, between what is functional for the system of dominant categories and what is dysfunctional for its political-discursive economy, was plotted in Chile as a concep-tual and semantic rupture. This rupture grew out of the challenge of having to name fragments of experience that were no longer speak-able in the language that survived the catastrophe of meaning. On the one hand was the fraudulent language spoken by the official power. On the other were the ideological mold of militant art serving the culture of political parties and the discourses of the social sciences, whose research format sought to frame the poetics of the crisis within an explanatory rationalism far removed from the instability of meanings unleashed by the critical juncture itself. Neither of these two languages was sufficiently sensitive to the turmoil of signs that had shaken the very machine of social representation.

The semantic and conceptual rupture to which Benjamin ap-pealed in his mention of refractory art (an art of negation and de-viation) was designed—in Chile—to escape military authoritarian-ism and the censorship administered by the official culture. But it also sought to escape certain ideological and technical forms of re-ductionism—the former, characterizing orthodox politics, and the latter, characterizing the sociology about oppositional culture. The more audacious and challenging works of the period attempted to break with the conformity of readings domesticated by the common-places of institutional rites, hegemonic traditions, militant creeds, official knowledge systems and their disciplinary hierarchies, the cul-tural market, and so on. It was necessary to reinvent "an indomi-table, irreducible, nongregarious reader": a reader faced with "com-municable but not easily processed"[9] signs, signs conserving in their interior a linguistic memory of the clashes born from repeated dis-armings of meaning. These clashes inscribed resistance and rebel-lion in the interior of the word, generating a memory of trauma in solidarity with the accidents and deformations of its graphing as a wounded word.

Recalling that word today as a zone of tensions and schisms is one way to keep from being deceived by the slogan of transparency that, in the name of the instrumental realism of consensus and of its sociocommunicative logic, attempts to file down every rough spot on the already too-polished and polite surface of the signs of agreement. Re-enabling that word as a field of plural and divergent forces is useful for opening it up to multiple points of view, whose contradictions should not remain silenced by the current desire to dissolve all opacity, to eliminate every strange body that threatens to obscure the vision of a cultural history falsely reconciled with itself.

The strange body that we must keep afloat, then, as a hybrid recollection, is one composed of "shreds of newspapers, fragments of extermination, syllables of death, pauses of untruth, commercial phrases, names of the deceased" that together speak, in a jumble, about the "infection of memory" that contaminated us through "a deep crisis of language, a disarticulation of all ideologies."[10] It is the impurity of that recollection that merits being made productive through a practice of memory unconcerned with the linear restitution of a single history, particularly given that the substance of history has been irreversibly contaminated by the suspicion weighing on every act presuming to represent a totality of meaning. This suspicion was activated by those aesthetic practices that had submitted the symbolic and discursive mediation of the categories of cultural thought to an intense critical revision, practices conjoined by the artistic and literary program Eugenia Brito called "a new scene of writing." It was this scene that, "much more powerfully than in previous periods,"[11] reconceptualized "the death of meaning, the cultural loss of the self, the barely regenerated suturing of gaps between the spaces, rhythms, and cadences in which one signifier replaces another, until arriving at the faintness of the last letter."[12]

In a text on Chilean art titled "Parpadeo y piedad," Pablo Oyarzún points out that, "around 1977, the question of photography became installed at the center of debates unfolding around and from within avant-garde activities."[13]

Debate during those years regarding the question of photography incorporated various levels of reflection, although one particularly heated controversy prevailed among groups within the Chilean artistic milieu. This polemic revisited arguments that reading "The Work of Art in the Age of Mechanical Reproduction" (1936) had made resonate, as weapons in a war of positions set off by the challenge of "*the politicization of art*" (Benjamin). It also tended to privilege—in response to that challenge—the documentary objectivity of photography (testimonial guarantee, denunciatory realism) above the imaginary transpositions and stylistic re-creations of painting, which were deemed too evocative. Certain aspects of this polemic suggested that incorporating visual technologies of mass reproduction into art condemned the "cultic" value of painting derived from its aura (contemplation, seclusion, mystery, eternity, etc.). They also suggested that the artisanship of the painting (a cult to individual talent cultivated by the manual nature of the trade) had been made obsolete by the technical modernity of the photograph, which relegated painting to a preindustry of the image. One part of Chilean postcoup art further raised a sort of ethical protest against the aesthetizing subjectivism of painting, accused of belonging "to the realm of self-absorption, self-expression, self-ishness," whose private quality made it seem complicit with the "act of 'pretending' certain things had not happened."[14] These were precisely the events that—by contrast—the camera could denounce, as a visual instrument unrivaled "for showing man in catastrophe."[15]

However, the works with the greatest reflexive density were those that led photographic documentation and pictorial representation to alternate and collate their critical-visual languages in the interior of the image itself. Both referred to a *crumbling of identity* on the stage of what Walter Benjamin called "an ultimate retrenchment: the human countenance."[16] The retrenchment of an "I" that—in the move from painted to photographic portraiture—exchanged the singular for the multiple, the original for the repeated, the authentic for the conventional, the purposeful for the arbitrary.

Certain critics (Ronald Kay, Enrique Lihn, and Adriana Valdés, among others) and certain artists (most especially, Eugenio Dittborn) investigated this situation of "the human countenance." A human face photographed by the machine of visual reproduction, to the point of extracting the analytical and metaphorical keys of a coercive plot, a plot that signaled procedures for *detaining* and *capturing* photographic identity: the prison of framing the shot, the straightjacket of the pose, the sentence of the montage, the prison term of the photo's edge, and so on. The detaining and capturing of an image whose imprisoning rhetoric underscored, by procedural analogy, the repressive control that every day affected those bodies submitted to the methods of military violence. The identification (ID) photograph spoke substitutionally of identity's own substitutions-destitutions, of the blackmailing and manipulation of roles that the social order exercised on those who were are obliged to identify themselves within its matrices of identification. Both the conversion of individual subjects into a "commonplace" of technical massification due to the stereotype of the pose and the deindividualization of individual subjects serialized by the genericness of a collective portrait archived at the Cabinet for Identification, provided the regulatory and classificatory basis of a system exercising its institutional power by taking possession *technically* of "an identity, as identified by the stereotyping machine" (Lihn). To speak of ID photos, then, was to speak about the identificatory molds and fittings that guaranteed the reproducibility of the order, regulating the pose. It was to expose the social conventions that governed identity based on a portrait-type as the model of disciplinary integration. But it was, above all, to convert the *identity on file* [*la identidad fichada*] typical of the portrait, into a *technical file card* [*ficha técnica*] typical of mechanisms for repressing identity, so that the victims of the repressive order could decipher its mediations of hidden signs in every attempt to erase the physical and symbolic mechanisms of this form of abuse.

When the family members of the detained-disappeared in Chile took to the streets exhibiting photographic portraits of those absent, they protested the Law, motivated by the knowledge that the enlarged photo—a photo ID—gave testimony to the first stigmatization of identity committed by the photographic apparatus: the sacrifice or evacuation of what is individual into a public mold.[17] When the Chilean artist Eugenio Dittborn amassed a countless number of anonymous, and therefore doubly deindividualized, photographs under the title "Fosa Común" [Common Grave] in a 1977 artwork, his work sketched a line of solidarity and union with family members of the detained-disappeared, communicating that he knew about the confiscation of identity exercised by agents of the State, and making known the impunity of their devices for erasing the traces of destruction [la traza del des-trozo] through an absence of names and signatures. Dittborn's work set up the similarity between portraits abandoned in the photographic shopwindow and bodies discarded by the machine of disidentity (torture + anonymity) in clandestine cemeteries. These were two situations in which portraits became the image of photographic denouncement in Chile. Such denouncement conceived of the photograph as a "crime scene" in which, according to Benjamin, the artist must "reveal guilt and . . . point out the guilty,"[18] following the technical footsteps of a visual machinery orchestrated by a serializing apparatus that dictates a collective verdict.

When Eugenio Dittborn, in his artistic production today, continues to unearth information buried in old photographs, disseminating it widely,[19] the artist makes visible a new form of solidarity with the detained-disappeared through the problem of bodies as trajectory and circulation: "Dittborn recirculates the image of subjects condemned to being forgotten" in order to show us how "the Chilean State attempted to take certain subjects out of circulation, condemning them to being forgotten."[20] He also does so to show us how recollection itself is en route to succumbing to forgetfulness, because the democratic slogan of looking ahead (of averting one's gaze from the conflicts of the past) once again makes the images of the missing disappear in the tomb of a non-present moment. Against the detained-disappeared's death by subtraction, which took the form of a retirement from circulation, Dittborn made the image of these bodies recirculate as a news item. And he did so when Chile had stopped being newsworthy on the ideological market of international solidarity culture, since democratic normalization had trivialized the tensions that served Chilean antidictatorial art as a contestatory emblem. Among other things, Dittborn's work posed the problem of the visibility and legibility of representations of memory as a zone where the relationships between concealment and disclosure—negotiated by certain reading priorities arranging the selection of what is representable and what is underreprcscntcd—might emerge.

The bursting open of plot in Dittborn's work is an expressive resource that sets up a visual (serigraphic) metaphor showing how a detail, amplified beyond the limits guaranteeing the clarity of its perception as part of a whole, makes the theme of memory explode: from *accumulation* to *dispersion*, from *saturation* to *disintegration*. The explosion of recollection (fragments, details) bursts memory's framework and alters those limits defining cultural representations and making them recognizable as a function of a socially composed and accepted repertoire.

But Dittborn's work further constructs another Benjaminian allegory of memory as *trace* and *reinscription*. His recovery of the news item (magazines in disuse like graves, and their exhuming) makes the image of what has been unearthed—the corpse of the dictatorship—function in a new signifying constellation, composed of many other submerged or shipwrecked identities (women, indigenous peoples, delinquents, the mentally ill), identities exchanging with that image their existential ruins, their vestiges of representation. The artwork sets up a configuration of subidentities that de-ideologize the portrait of the Victim of the Dictatorship, mobilizing its image outside official catalogs. And joining it together—in fresh associations—with more dispersed fragments and the (still) unfound remains of various collapses and submergings that speak about residual subjectivities and drifting codes.

Minds astray in different regions of human biography (infancy, old age) or of social pathology (insanity, delinquency), and bodies afloat at the different latitudes of lives in extinction (from the aborigines of the Tierra del Fuego to the mummy at Cerro del Plomo, passing through the detained-disappeared of the dictatorship), together construct a large collective portrait with many disassembled pieces of identity. This is a genealogical portrait in which the *nonsynchronous* (different social and historical temporalities separated by chasms of distance), the *disqualified* (the minor, the subaltern), and the *heterogeneous* (the nonidentical, the nonuniform) progressively indicate that the only identity surviving the Chile of the dictatorship, that can be reconstructed today, is that identity tying together—loosely, with ellipses—archaisms and modernity, vital forces and collapses in meaning, memories and events misplaced in time.

MEMORY AND DISCONTINUITY

The postcoup Chilean landscape revealed the dislocation of that referential horizon, drawn by tradition and the past as one of historical continuity. However, many practices—hypersensitized to the effect of cuts by the fracturing and dispersive mark of that rupture of horizons—sought to recover from that breaking of languages by weaving together codes for keeping alive the illusion that history and tradition were reconstructable continuities, despite the abruptness of their interruption. That tendency to rehistoricize the past, as a depository of the values of national and popular identity to be rescued and protected for the sake of communal integration, characterized various Chilean manifestations of a culture of solidarity and militancy still committed to the ideological referents of the classical left. Those manifestations were dedicated to the suturing and reparation of a broken continuity, through the creation of expressive ties with tradition. These ties, in turn, were destined to *refamiliarize* the art public with its cultural legacy in order to remedy the effects of *alienation* caused by a traumatic surging forth of the disfigured and the irreconcilable within the dictatorship's field of historical vision. Especially in theater, the works with the greatest cultural resonance (taking the group ICTUS as the paradigm) defended the necessity of protecting the historicity of a cultural patrimony threatened with disintegration, emphasizing the play's character as a "*rite*" through which "spectators recognize themselves as part of a community of shared values, historical experiences, symbolic universes, and consensually recognized social identities."[21]

But such "*historical thought*, saturated with experience,"[22] which recurred to an exemplary past as the value reserve for a national identity transmitted through the languages of tradition, did not constitute the only alternative response to the crisis of references and significations that had dismantled the cultural universe. There also appeared what Rodrigo Cánovas called—apropos of Enrique Lihn's literature—"*satirical thought*":[23] an uninhibited way of thinking that critiqued "the cultural order" by putting into practice "a discourse of reflexivity, attentive to its own programming, and based on self-parody."[24] That discourse—"which placed in question the very act of conceptualizing anything through language"[25]—was the tendency characterizing the most strongly deconstructive works to appear during the authoritarian period. These were works that, above and beyond the banner of protest-denunciation, were able to rediagram critical utopias by raising their precise, precious, and rebellious vocabularies against the totalizing discourses of ideological thought.

These insurgent vocabularies found memory to be a first territory to reconquer. But they did not proceed with their reconquest by following those who symbolized the past through historicist monuments to continuity, as a *plenum* of meaning and a transcendental horizon of truths to be recovered in the name of victims still trusting redemptive solutions. Instead, facing the official deceit of a past distorted by the historical fraud of the seizure of power, and facing the nostalgia of that other past sublimated—in its inverse—by the continuism of ideological discourse, various works sought to delegitimate the traditions of the Past using the subterfuge of denouncing—through parody—what each discipline had ritualized as its heritage, linguistic patrimony, and conventions. In art, revisions by Chilean artists Eugenio Dittborn, Carlos Altamirano, and Gonzalo Díaz[26] disrupted the academic legacy of the national pictorial tradition as a first subsystem of falsities and falsifications to question and reformulate. The works of these three Chilean artists depaginated the historical-national sequence of the official art tradition by interrupting it with the *memories-in-negative* censored and repressed by its canonical past. Memories associated with the subaltern registers of the domestic and the popular, the urban, the feminine, and the biographical-erotic, entered as contraband into the upper regions of cultural representation, to contest the hierarchies of race, class, and gender fixing the scale of distinctions and privileges consecrated by traditional art.

Chilean poetry and narrative of the same period also took on the task of excising hegemonic narrations, of fissuring them with words hostile to the claims of official truth. Such claims were threatened as authors filled them with doubts, using "ellipses, repetitions, interstices through which the signifier makes visible its defects and deprivations,"[27] as well as gaps in argumentation. Diego Maquieira's *La tirana* [The Woman Tyrant] (1983) breaks the mold of the Spanish language of the Conquest, with an orgiastic mixture of contrary idioms that assail it from below, from underneath. The Spanish of tradition, which forms the cultured and religious memory of Latin American society, is transgressed by the "ferocious ordinariness" (Maquieira) of citations whose dissonant alterity celebrates the struggle of textualities that shred the referent of the mother tongue. *Este* [East] by Gonzalo Muñoz (1983) recurs to the figure of disjuncture in order to stage an account of History as a memory of broken links, dispersed fragments, and multiple and contradictory series: a memory capable of being recreated only through an uneven chorus of hybrid voices, in which origins and pasts escape the foundational hierarchy of a unique word. Diamela Eltit's *Por la patria* [For the Fatherland] (1986) fills its narration with contradictory and mutually conflicting sub-accounts to raise suspicion regarding the central story's monologue, crisscrossing its narrative cues to the point of frustrating any overarching synthesis and diverting the historicist's linear push toward preprogrammed resolutions.

All of these works illustrate the Benjaminian idea that "history's continuity is that of the oppressors," while "the history of the oppressed is discontinuous": an unfinished succession of loose fragments unleashed by cuts in meaning, and wandering about, without the guarantee of a sure connection or an exact end. For these works, both the act of recollection (of practicing historical memory) and the act of interpretation (of rehearsing formulas for comprehending reality) imply placing the various events and their narrations in confrontation with one another, in order to open up the story of experience and the experience of the story to discontinuous and multiply crossed readings that could denounce the trap of rationalizations based on complete truths and absolute rationality. Only a precarious narrative of the *residual* was capable of staging the decomposition of general perspectives, centered visions, and finished portraits: a narrative that only "lets scraps of language be heard, remnants of signs,"[28] pulling together misplaced threads and misappropriated words.

The Benjaminian critique of History's homogenous linearity and univocal directionality resonated in those images from Chilean postcoup culture that accentuated "negativity, discontinuity, rejection, and clashes."[29] Only such a critique of monologic totalizations, made from the plural constellations of dispersed significations, could enter into a complicity of styles with social imaginaries disintegrated by ruptures in the chain of a historical macrosyntagm.

AESTHETICS OF THE DISCARD

Benjamin's antihistoricist criticism was aimed at the heroic monumentality of capitalized Truths. He carried it out using fine details of small events that crumbled significations, often viewed by chroniclers of transcendent history as if they were materials to discard. An admirer of portions and shards of experience that relate to the Whole—not from a position of knowledge confident in its plenitude, but rather from the splintering word of its dis-integrity—Walter Benjamin would have recognized himself in the geographies of the fragment certain Chilean voices traced. Voices that were multiplied through fissures in the monological subject both of the official tradition's *authorship/authority* and of military culture's *authoritarianism*.

We know that "the popular Latin American *testimonio* . . . arises in circumstances in which life has suffered irreversible changes and is on the way toward *reconstruction*. And it is precisely the testimonial modality that becomes one of the privileged vehicles for that reconstruction" of life,[30] due to its capacity to model new forms of expression and local constructions of subjectivities in crisis. In fact, the Chile of the dictatorship made the testimonio a privileged format that "gave voice to the voiceless," textualizing life stories and biographical narrations situated at the margins of those visions constituted and institutionalized through the master narratives of the social sciences and politics. Testimonio—as a subjectivized instance of "knowledge that demythologizes the 'totality' "[31]—proposes a *situated* capturing of the real (relative, partial) that corrects the totalizing gaze of a macrosocial focus. But despite that partializing and relativizing quality of testimonial speech, which seeks to refute the universal fiction of an absolute subject, those exponents of testimonio that monopolized the attention of Chilean sociology during the period of reconstructing memory and national identity continued to portray characters (the political victim, the woman, the indigenous person, etc.) whose marginality and oppression symbolized a national consciousness sustained by the communal paradigm of denouncement, no matter how fractured its enunciative viewpoint.

However, on the most frayed edges of the testimonial genre's ethical-narrative plot, valorized by Chilean sociology as a *document* (that is, as proof and lesson), arose other experimentations that evaded the consciousness-raising imperative of life narratives. This imperative had been ciphered in "the redemption of popular voices, the syntax and cosmovision of the oppressed" through "a gaze attempting to construct 'a truth' from the perspective of the most marginal protagonists of history."[32] Situated on the periphery of a "truth" already cataloged and recovered by the sociology of marginality, the new aesthetics of the testimonio did not seek to fill gaps in identity with consoling words. Instead, it preferred to expose— in those gaps—the absence of a whole, the lack itself, and to re-aestheticize that lack as a *de-figuration* of the whole through "figures at the abyss, emptied of all interiority"[33] that no longer reached the confirming weight of a valorized referentiality serving, protectively, as a guide for social consciousness. The urban vagabond in Diamela Eltit's El padre mío [Father of Mine] (1989) and the transvestite prostitutes in Claudia Donoso and Paz Errázuriz's La manzana de Adán / Adam's Apple (1990)[34] embodied this register of dis-identity through a frenetic assembling of intercutting and disguised voices. Here, madness and deprivation painted themselves in variegated styles—overloaded themselves with ornaments—in order to take revenge on a nation condemned to the misery of the nonsensical. Bodies without a residence or belongings, and subjects lacking interiority or content (dispossessed of the essence of an identity-property), configured "presences structured in appearance only, following a complex and torn cosmetic order" that permitted "glimpses of multiple significations, from the multiplicity of additives that composed the violent exteriority to which they had been reduced."[35] That "violent exteriority" was part of a suburban map in whose borders of trafficking and clandestine activities came together the inhabitants of "zones of pain, crime, insanity, sex for sale; hospitals, hospices, asylums, jails, and whorehouses; plazas, soda fountains, and public restrooms; the freeways entering and leaving the city, and the barren areas."[36] These sites—as places of crime and infraction—set up a scenographic explosion of mad compulsions within the marginal zones. The lack of property and identity of these subjects, extremely variable and mobile—"constantly moving around and changing their names, clothing, sex," and speech[37]—placed emphasis on mutations of identity and on transferences of gender/genre that destabilized the function of testimonio, understood as the collective vector of identity-based representations. By contrast to what occurred with the existential emphasis on content characteristic of the ideology of testimonio favored by alternative sociology, Diamela Eltit's El padre mío was delirious with "appearance and exteriority" as a cosmetic splintering of the baroque machinery saturating signs with variegated forms and textures.

The found forms (rubbish dumps) of speech characteristic of those subjects roaming along the outskirts of the city's cartography experienced sophisticated cuts and montages that could account for the "collective," not as a mass, but rather as a flow to partition and reassemble in new connections and intensities. Appearances luxuriously overloaded using a technique of aesthetic supplements configured these identities-simulacra, adorning the Chilean punishment of deprivation with a superabundance of excess. These identities-simulacra thereby exhibited a signic search for metaphors of deterioration, incrusting their luster with the syntagm of poverty. The exhibitionistic squandering of this cosmetics of desire could only bear the mark of an aesthetic perversion for those believers in the ethics of the testimonio and in its social referentiality as political protest. The explanatory and verifying logic of its sociological frame found itself violently convulsed by the spasms of identity unleashed in its interior by works like Eltit's in literature and Errázuriz's in photography. These works invaded—and keep invading—the shores of the irrational and nonsensical (classified as "madness" by social norms), in order to deploy the trembling symptom of precariousness in all of its metaphorical extension.

The "reaccentuation of genres" Bakhtin spoke about became formalized in these Chilean works as the twisted de-generation of both discursive genres and sexual genders. Testimonio already had taken on the task of questioning the hierarchizing of genres defended by the canonical tradition of institutionalized literature. But it was now documentary language's turn to become transfigured under the influence of Chilean women writers' cosmetic voices. Retouched voices that hyperfictionalized the representational "truth" of testimonio, twisting and contorting gender-sexuality (femininity, transvestism), and thus submitting the militaristic and patriarchal pattern of dominant identity, and its regimenting masculinity, to blackmail and extortion.

"By focusing on the fragmentary nature of experience and by leaving aside the impulse to totalize,"[38] the testimonial genre already had called into question the monologic voice of any author who interpreted the social narrative from a position of superior knowledge supported in macro-units of signification. But this was not enough. The Chilean dictatorship pushed the fragmentariness of the testimonio toward new extremes of creativity, in which stylistic maneuvers, technical subterfuges, and fictional artifices perfected a sub-version of the genre, in order to give a much-deserved eloquence to that "in-essential, disposable 'I' " embraced by Benjamin: shred of identity, narrative residue, lexical discard, technological rubbish, sexual errata, and the failing of genres and genders.

REINVENTING MEMORY, TODAY

To turn the page, to close the chapter: these are some of the images that surround the theme of the dictatorship's past (the violation of human rights) today, figuring memory as book, narrative, and archive. This reference to books conserves the metaphor of a volume of writings in which arranged meanings are deposited for future consultation. But the arrangement of these meanings may find itself altered and de-composed, as the account and its narration set in motion novel forms of recombining time and sequences, of alternating pauses and flashbacks, of anticipating endings and skipping over beginnings, through a reading that resists being so predictably subordinated to the chronology of linear time. Such a chronology keeps captive as past what is stored there, until certain temporal disjunctures release the nexes in a programmed continuity. The present then becomes a disjunctive knot, capable of making recollection not a return to the past (a regression that buries history in the recesses of yesterday), but rather a coming and going along the winding turns of a memory that does not stop at fixed points, passing instead along a critical multidirectionality of nonpacted alternatives.§ Gonzalo Díaz referred to this in his installation "Lonquén 10 años" [Lonquén 10 Years] (1989), through the "fragmented obscurities that we string together to illuminate an event," or through "a distortion that art can barely name."[39] The Lonquén massacre—"a pestilent *punctum* that stubbornly surfaces from within the dense marsh of a monotonous official discourse"—came to light and public knowledge thanks to the way in which Gonzalo Díaz's work effectively "poked art's finger into the sore spot of politics."[40]

The Chilean return to democracy constructed a staging of discourses around the problem of memory, figured principally as a tension between forgetting (burying the past of unburied bodies: *re-*

covering) and recollection (exhuming that which covers—veils—that past: *dis-covering*). But the turns of memory rely on mechanisms that are much more intertwined and overlapping than those consigned by this duality of contrary processes. Once one has discarded "the amnesiac smoothing out of history, which is, among other things, an offense to the present,"[41] the work of memory may be reimagined. It may be reconceived not as a passive memory of an objectified recollection, but as a memory-subject capable of formulating constructive and productive ties between past and present, in order to make explode that "now-time" (Benjamin's *Jetztzeit*) retained and compressed within the historical particles of many discrepant recollections, previously silenced by an official memory. This work of recollection has been cause for reflection within various cultural practices in postdictatorial Chile, which have taken it on, pursuing diverse rhythms and inspirations. Together, these practices provide certain aesthetic-critical counterpoints suggesting conflicting representations of the relationship between history and memory. This is what occurred, to take theater as an example, with two works that raked through the sediments of the same past of the dictatorship, recharting its imprint on the present democratic transition, but with deeply conflicting representational devices. The works in question are Ariel Dorfman's *La muerte y la doncella* [*Death and the Maiden*][42] and Alfredo Castro's *Teatro de la memoria* [Theater of Memory].[43]

In Dorfman's case, the problem of the role of memory was articulated through tropes that recited the political libretto of Chilean society during the democratic transition. Actions and characters became established in conformity with, and reiterating, forms of logic within the repertoire of conflicts sanctioned by the official discourse at that political juncture. The theatrical subject matter revolved around the same dualities and oppositions that had been part of the rhetoric created by the human rights agenda: victim/victimizer, harm/reparation, offense/pardon, and so on. No enunciative unsettling or significant rupture sought to disorganize the series of figurations by which history and memory were symbolized in accordance with the terms established by the dominant narrative. The play protected the *order* and *composition* of meanings negotiated—and granted — by the regime's official version during the democratic transition, safeguarding the hierarchy of certain overarching referents that remained fully intact, without a verbal trace of alteration or deterioration. The representational guarantee of the theatrical message was firmly supported by the relationship of equivalency between signifier and signified through which the play continued to enable the ideologemes of social and political realism characteristic of that historical juncture, without exposing them to larger conflicts in their verbalization.

Meanwhile, Alfredo Castro elaborated a "theater of memory" spoken in a language crushed by the violent clashes and disconnections that had broken the sequential aspects of names and things. Castro's syntactic disabling of referential discourse frustrated every identificatory projection (in contrast to what occurred with Dorfman) and subverted the dualistic axis of the negative-positive through diffuse ambivalences, through truncated phrases disarming the ideological-communicative conventions of the theatrical message with their erratic dispunctuation. The archeology of memory in Castro's theater made fragments of consciousness collide, juxtaposed in disorder, thereby preventing any meaning of history from resting on a precomposed structure. The metalevel of recollection's inscription-fixation, as a topic of memory in the drama of identity, was inverted by a disconnected gesticulation of bodies and biographies in pieces that had broken the ties of verbal syntagms in order to explore — tentatively — the substrata of social representation's discursive formalizations.

The international press has conjectured widely about the relative lack of success of Dorfman's play in Chile when it was staged for the first time in 1991, as compared with its subsequent success in England and the United States.[44] The most widespread commentary was that the Chilean public was not prepared to receive, elaborate on, and process the traumatic burden of that recollection of the dictatorship dramatized in the play. But the frustrated act of its Chilean reception could stimulate another type of commentary.

Why not think instead that this play, planned outside Chile, failed here because it did not incorporate into its construction — it had no way of doing so—a certain fatigue produced among us by the many ideologized discourses conveying the vanquished's standpoint as a "fatally rectilinear succession of victory and defeat" (Adorno)?

In order critically to twist the ideological linearity of that "standpoint of the vanquished," it was necessary to be able—just as Adorno himself had proposed in his essay on Benjamin—"to address . . . things which were not embraced by this dynamic, which fell by the wayside—what might be called the waste products and blind spots that have escaped the dialectic."[45] Blind spots that demand an aesthetic of diffuse lighting, so that their forms acquire the indirect meaning of what is shown obliquely, of that which circulates along the narrow paths of recollection, filtered by barely discernible fissures of consciousness.

Part of the critical task incumbent on postdictatorial thought is to overcome the rigid dichotomy of values and representations imprisoning "the standpoint of the vanquished" by exploring more oblique forms, together with resolving the conflict between assimilating (incorporating) or expelling (rejecting) the past. Critically resolving this conflict means as much avoiding the nostalgia of an antidictatorial Symbol, as it does resisting any enterprise of forgetfulness that seeks to reunify history by forcibly appeasing those forces disputing its meaning. The artistic and cultural practices that worked to reelaborate the most tortuous meanings of historical memory are those best prepared to intervene in this conflictive theater of recollection, restaging—in a roundabout way—what "fell by the wayside": interrupted sequences and inconclusive fragments still hidden in the seams of the triumphant discourses of reconstruction, in the folds and reverses that continue to distrust the glorious ends of the finished phrase and phase.

TWO

A Border Citation:

Between Neo– and Post–Avant-Garde

A look at national artistic development indicates how "the evolution of art in Chile, since the end of the fifties, can be described as a series of modernizations."[1] There has emerged "a self-conscious modernity of art organized . . . as a field of inquiries and executions" that seek to impact "every node in the circuit of artistic production: the artwork, the producer, the public, the multiple relationships between them, the institutional fixing of these relationships, [and] the determinations of art itself and of its link to the real."[2]

The gradual progression of this order was violently shaken after 1973, when artistic movements, aesthetic programs, and cultural forces had to abandon the pretense of engaging linear correspondences of signs, because the interreferentiality of the series "art," "society," "culture," "modernity," and so forth, had been dislocated by breaks in the historical and political totality.

An experimental Chilean group, the *Colectivo de Acciones de Arte* [Art Actions Collective, henceforth CADA] protagonized this scene of dislocation when it enacted a border citation of neo–avant-garde art in the convulsed landscape of the dictatorship. It did so at a time when transformations in society already suggested a rupture in the ideas of totality and totalization that had sustained the avant-garde critique of both the artistic and the social system's dominant ideology.

The group CADA formed part of the Chilean artistic scene referred to as the *escena de avanzada*.[3] Constituted after 1977, its most polemic stance developed from the critical radicalism of linguistic experimentation vehemently directed against the art-system. The escena de avanzada developed a range of aesthetic proposals that shared, among other traits, "the exigency of demonstrating in the work an analytical lucidity about the social and ideological conditionality of its own exercise" and "a tense logic of confrontation between its marginal *status* (and its will to marginality) and its various institutionalized manifestations."[4]

The set of socio-aesthetic reformulations that the *avanzada* proposed was made explicit around the following cuts and fractures:

— The dismantling of "the painting" as artwork and of its ritualized contemplation (the sacralized aura, the unique work's fetishization, etc.). This was achieved through a critique of the Fine Arts' aristocratic tradition, accompanied by a social reinsertion of the image in the serial and reproductive context of visual mass culture (documentary photography, news reports) and of popular culture's subgenres (comic strips, soap operas).

— The questioning of institutional frameworks for validating and consecrating the "masterpiece" (histories of art, the Museum) and of the circuits for commercializing the work-product (galleries). This was accomplished through practices like performance or video installations that deconstructed the reifying tradition of artistic consumption.

— The transgression of discursive genres. This occurred through works that combined various systems of sign production (texts, images, gestures) and that exceeded technical and formal specificities, mixing cinema and literature, art and sociology, aesthetics and politics, in an interdisciplinary way.

All of the works that comprised the avanzada participated in that same rupturistic cut. But CADA exacerbated that cut by reemphasizing the avant-garde call to bridge and fuse the domains of art, politics, and society.

Created in 1979, the group CADA was composed of two writers (Raúl Zurita and Diamela Eltit), a sociologist (Fernando Balcells), and two visual artists (Lotty Rosenfeld and Juan Castillo). Despite the later disintegration of this founding group, throughout its history CADA maintained the same productive tension resulting from the combination of several registers: cultural (art, literature), social (the urban body as a zone of intervention in the collective biography), and political (its link with forces of social change mobilized by the left).

CADA's principal works in the culminating phase of the avanzada were two: "Para no morir de hambre en el arte" [1979, So as Not to Die of Hunger in Art] and "¡Ay Sudamérica!" [1981, Oh, South America!].

"So as Not to Die of Hunger in Art" consisted of the following interventions enacted simultaneously:

— Chilean artists distribute one hundred liters of milk to families in a Santiago shantytown.
— One page in the popular magazine Hoy [Today] is diverted from its journalistic function to become an enunciative support of the work, with the following text: "Imagine this page completely blank / imagine this blank page as white as milk for daily consumption / imagine all corners of Chile deprived of milk for daily consumption as blank pages to be filled."
— A text recorded in five languages is read in front of the United Nations building in Santiago, situating Chile under the sign of its precarious and marginal condition within the international panorama.
— An acrylic box is sealed at the art gallery Centro Imagen. It contains bags of milk not distributed among the population, together with a copy of Hoy and a tape of the text read in front of the UN. The milk remains there until it decomposes, with the message: "To remain here until our people are able to gain access to basic food for consumption. To remain as the symbolic inverse of a lacking, inverted, plural body."

— Ten milk trucks parade through the city, departing from a milk factory (representing the food production industry) and arriving at a conservative art center (the Museum).

— An expanse of white canvas is hung over the entrance to the Museum, metaphorically suggesting an act of institutional closure.

Performed two years later, in an equally collective manner, CADA's work "Oh, South America!" entailed dropping 400,000 fliers from three airplanes over impoverished sectors of Santiago. They carried the following statement: "The work of improving the accepted standard of living is the only valid project for art / the only exhibition / the only worthwhile artwork. Everyone who works, if only mentally, to expand the spaces in his or her life is an artist."

CADA's two works demonstrated principal avant-garde emblems through certain programmatic devices, such as the use of the *pamphlet* as a theoretico-discursive accompaniment and propagandistic support, one that multiplies those effects most characteristic of the genre's rhetoric: predicatory, exhortative, militant, utopian, consciousness raising, prophesying, and so on. There are two longings for vindication transmitted by the principal avant-garde emblems cited by CADA: the fusion *art/life* and the fusion *art/politics*.

The Fusion Art/Life

As Peter Bürger has stated, "[w]e have works of art because we have the institution"[5] that classifies them as such. That is, art is socially valued as art due to the institutional discourses (histories of art, the museum, etc.) that trace the symbolic and material boundaries responsible for assigning a value to the work's artistry and circumscribing it within a particular frame of aesthetic differentiation. Proof of this is given by Duchamp's "Urinal" (1919), which simultaneously *highlights* and *problematizes* the *conventionality* of the limit between art and non-art. If the artistic institution is the normative frame that socially defines what is art and consecrates it as such, one must attack that institution to revolutionize the meaning and function of art, exploding the boundaries that divorce it from life.

When CADA, in "So as Not to Die of Hunger in Art," effaces the facade of the Museo Nacional de Bellas Artes [National Fine Arts Museum] with a stretch of canvas that virtually blocks the entrance, it censures artistic institutionality in two ways. It censures this monument first as *Museum* (an allegory of art's sacralizing tradition in the past) and, second, as *Chilean* Museum (a symbol of the cultural officialism of the dictatorship). But it does so while at the same time reclaiming the street as "the true Museum," in which the everyday trajectories of the city's inhabitants become—through an inversion of the gaze—the new works of art to be contemplated. The mobile temporality of the street is the open and site-specific format of a work-happening that responds to the dead (static) time of Museum paintings. This emphasis on the street "expands the art public's reality toward that massive realm habitually excluded from [art],"[6] and denounces the elitist convention of sequestering painting within art's selective interior. To break with the foreclosure of art's interiority (its inner walls) and accomplish the avant-garde goal of art's incorporation into life's exteriority, the divisions that render art *incommunicable*—the walls of a room (= the confinement of art and the institution as closure)—must be abolished. For the horizontal exchange of the signs "art" and "life" to occur, the features of superiority and exceptionality that *distinguish* (highlight and favor) the privative meaning of art must also be eliminated. In CADA's pieces, the book's page fades until it finally merges with the Chilean landscape that displaces and replaces it. The image of the author is deindividuated to the point that it is lost—multiplied—into anonymity: "Everyone who works, if only mentally, to expand the spaces in his or her life is an artist." Echoing the concepts elaborated by the German artist Wolf Vostell, CADA declared that the artist "simply works with experience" and that artworks are nothing more than "life reformulated," the critical transformation of everyday experience into aesthetic substance.

The avant-garde call to live art as an integral fusion of aesthetics and everyday life implies overcoming the material and symbolic confines of the artistic institution and "dismantling the Manichaean notion of art's alterity to life."[7] It implies reconciling art and life into a *whole* without divisions or compartmentalization. The division of languages and compartmentalization of spheres and values are seen as responsible—by that artistic avant-garde—for reinforcing the internal logic of each practice, forcing the foreclosure of self-referentiality. "The impugnment of both art's self-referentiality and the concept of specific practice"[8] sought by CADA demands the dissolution of the values of artistic autonomy and specificity fixed by the limits that separate and regulate the distance between reality (life) and discourse (art). The elimination of every limit used to differentiate between *code* (the mediation of the sign) and *experience* (the im-mediacy of the real) is the necessary condition to achieve art's "utopian (metaphysical or revolutionary) reintegration" into the continuum of existence,[9] without the interruption of a semiotic-cultural system of punctuation that might imply a cut or separation. That avant-garde utopia shared by CADA is one of a fused continuity of experience seeking to transcend the dis-continuity of signs that intervene in the real, "delimiting fields of action, formalizing social relationships, [and] institutionalizing processes of interaction"[10] with separatist rites and differentiating norms.

The Fusion Art/Politics

CADA became an artistic group at a time when the dictatorial universe was dominated by an *adherence to limits*, both symbolic and territorial. The *move-beyond-the-frame [salida-de-marco]* put into practice by the works of the avanzada constituted a metaphorical critique of the dictatorial *frame-ing [en-marque]* that sought to confine and segregate both bodies and the discursive order. It took as its point of departure a transgression of the pictorial conventions of painting: a transgression that was simultaneously an aggressive assault on the laws reducing everything to redoubts (disciplines and specificities), laws that compartmentalize and isolate cultural practices. CADA's gesture bore the stamp of "an avant-garde rebellion in response to the radical claim for autonomy made by the aestheticism" of art for art's sake.[11]

Against the bourgeois assumption of "an aesthetics of autonomy," CADA advanced the militancy of a socially committed art that sought to transcend restrictive definitions of art and politics, inscribing itself in the tradition of a certain Latin American avant-garde that appeared to have demonstrated, according to CADA, that it already was "possible to understand both collective objectives (a class-free society) and the militancy for those objectives, as art-actions, that is, as artworks."[12]

For CADA, the ideologues' refrain that "everything is political" was "transformed into a vehement 'everything is art'"[13] that demanded the absence of all limits (discursive boundaries) because each limit was perceived as a *limitation* to be abolished. An absence of limits formulated the utopia of the limit-less, affirming a belief in an all-powerful art capable of exceeding any regulatory division. This art would represent "the collapse of every form of limitation,"[14] creating a salvational utopia or a macroliberty that "could overcome all forms of conditioning"[15] and that could transcend all forms of dependency and subjection. It envisioned a kind of space *beyond* the rules articulating—and regulating—human praxis, as Raúl Zurita proposed in the manifesto accompanying his "Escrituras en el cielo" [Sky Writing] realized in 1982 in New York.

The avant-garde militancy of CADA led it, on the one hand, to define itself as a "revolutionary force" that counted on art—and aesthetic mediums—for setting in motion the social processes of a collective coming to awareness and liberation. But it also led CADA to join a more global project that could orient and *justify*—lend legitimacy to—its artistic practice; the work "established its effectiveness through the general perspective of the construction of a different order."[16] That general perspective was marked by the work's sociohistorical and teleological horizon, which overdetermined its meaning, transposing it to the macro dimension of a series of structural changes across all of society. Artistic judgment regarding the validity of the work—and corroborated by the historical sanctioning of social transformation—depended on its efficient contribution to the materialization of these changes. For its authors, "the proposal, then, of art-actions as an 'Art of History'" must be understood with all its consequences: "its success or failure is not detached from the success or failure of perspectives regarding the total alteration of society."[17] Those visionary considerations regarding art's role as a precursor in anticipating social change rested on a conception of history oriented toward end goals, and seen as a linear, evolutionary march toward the plenitude of achieved results. A march driven by the rationalization of the process converted into unequivocal law, based on the emancipatory role of the "working class, bearer of history,"[18] whose revolutionary ascent culminates in "the production of a classless society."[19]

CADA's artistic-revolutionary call reiterated the tendency toward *no division* as a totalizing principle of universal categorization. Just as the synthesis art/life proposed the real as an *undifferentiated* whole (with no formal limit between experiential and discursive regimes), the fusion art/politics proposed the social and historical as *unified* totalities: history as a *plenum* of meaning in the service of a final and transcendent referent, and society as a macro-horizon capable of absorbing difference and resolving contradictions, once the utopia of the homogenous (indivisible) body of "the classless society" became concrete.

NEO–AVANT-GARDE CITATION
AND HORIZONS OF THE "POST"

The dislocated landscape of the Chilean dictatorship was the horizon for CADA's neo–avant-garde citation—a landscape whose subversive zones were inhabited by distinct forces and directionalities of meaning that sought to resignify the crisis using alternative vocabularies.

In CADA's case, despite the programmatic drive of its own discourse, one could already find a certain discordance in the formulation of the relationship between art and society underlying its works. The problematic fit between theoretical postulation (CADA's program) and aesthetic materialization (its "art-actions") suggested an ambivalence of meaning: while the theoretical program defended a totalization of the social for staging the global transformations embraced by the work's content, the "art-actions" *de-multiplied* that totality when they intervened in its signifying planes in a *segmentary* way. This is what occurred in "So as Not to Die of Hunger in Art" when trucks parading through the streets, milk exhibited in the gallery, a page taken over in a magazine, a Museum entrance covered, and so forth, created a series of local alterations to the urban plot. These were produced *in segments* and therefore belied the maximizing figure of the "total system." Many other ambivalences in the postulates contained in CADA's work already suggested a first bifurcation of the postdictatorship Chilean gaze in the relationship between art, politics, and society. On the one hand—and without a doubt, this proved the most overt—the texts made avant-garde utopianism resonate with its foundational and messianic echoes, which projected a future redeemed through the abolition of all divisions; on the other, the works set forth a "situational and situated art" that multiplied *localized* actions at different *points of intersection* in the socio-institutional plot.

The escena de avanzada was further split between CADA's neo–avant-garde formulation and other practices that distanced themselves from its messianic utopianism. While CADA opted to respond to the violence of Chilean social disintegration by reinforcing the cohesive and integrating synthesis of the Totality (the *whole* of society as the artistic revolution's macro-domain), other practices—Leppe, Dittborn, Altamirano, Díaz, and Brugnoli-Errázuriz, among others —worked on the erratic quality of fragments and "the disillusioning memory of discards,"[20] those remaining bits of meaning in precarious transitings that escaped the grandiloquence of great, all-encompassing syntheses. Their works—which sought to "deinstall all unifying gazes" (Brugnoli)—were in frank disagreement with the globalizing images of history and society under which CADA attempted to subsume artistic practice. That deinstallation of the gaze put into practice in works by Leppe, Dittborn, Altamirano, Díaz, and Brugnoli-Errázuriz, was complicitous with the fractured identities of a broken biography, *deemphasizing* CADA's heroic monumentalist tendency and its revolutionary emblems of a universal truth attributed to historical consciousness. This universalism hinged on the proletarian model as a "witnessing subject/operator" destined—according to Gonzalo Muñoz—to carry out "the symbolic reappropriation of life and its spaces, in an attempt to dominate, in its meaning, the savage shape of the present . . . and formulate through the potency of history a desired future."[21] While CADA imagined life as art's informal (unstructured) underside, these other practices warded off the naturalist myth by emphasizing reality as the semiotic product of discursive artifice and by operating on the real in terms of syntactic *discontinuity, fragmentation, and montage*. While CADA subordinated art to the broad terms of a transparent and homogenous society, these other practices staged the failure of those ascending linearities and the weakening of meaning through disconnected sequences of fragmentary and dispersed micronarratives.

These differing propositions, from the utopian-revolutionary avant-garde's rupturistic tendencies cited by CADA to the deconstructivist criticism of post–avant-garde art, were part of a complex landscape in which changes to ideological-cultural sensibility were occurring. These changes were marked by three enterprises: (1) *destruction* (the homicidal violence of the military intervention); (2) *reconstruction* (the resymbolization of a communal nexus as a force behind national identity); and (3) *deconstruction* (the appearance of a "discourse of the crisis" [Cánovas] that learned to be skeptical of all efforts to remonumentalize history).

Two tendencies within the avanzada staged alternative models for conceptualizing the relationships between art and social critique. The first, along the lines of the avant-garde, vindicated the aesthetic project as the link among forces for change seeking to transform the full range of social structures. The second, along the lines of postmodernist critiques of avant-garde ideologies, sought to design partial operations capable of altering and subverting the system through the micrological play of *situated* actions.

No matter how mistaken "the usual equation of the avant-garde with modernism"[22] may be, that equation has led us to think that "what these days goes by the name of postmodernism could more accurately be termed a post-avant-garde."[23] In fact, the crisis of the avant-garde has been one of the principal references of the postmodernism debate. The first avant-garde assumption challenged by postmodernism is its radical faith in an absolute counter-institutionality. The heretical figure of a call against order was reiterated by the avant-garde through the antibourgeois dimension of provocation and scandal. However, the ability with which the system of conventions (taste, tradition) was capable of reinserting iconoclastic gestures into a reasoned catalog of permissible deviations—in this way neutralizing the challenge, and reeducating the transgressive turn as a normalized form, courtesy of the market—prompted the first suspicions about the radical myth of institutional transgression.

Postmodernism's suspicions also reached the avant-garde ideology of progress, which sought to destroy the regressive symbols of the academy or of institutions, liquidating every tie with the past. This exacerbated a dialectic of continuity-rupture that resolved any gaps with the intransigent form of a foundational cut. The postmodern categories of the asynchronic and discontinuous refute the historicist continuity of that avant-garde logic based on an evolutionary trajectory of advances and improvements, arguing instead for the failure of uniform rationalities. Such a failure cancels the metaphysical value of an ascending history guided by an ultimate end that overdetermines its course. In the case of the avant-garde, the end anticipated by its explosion of languages was social revolution. To overthrow order, as a metaphor of the institution safeguarding the system, was the anarchist banner of an art motivated by the revolutionary utopia of a global transformation of society. Postmodern criticism refutes this totalizing formula of the avant-garde, which subordinated the artwork to the transcendent metajustification of a redemptive signified. And it proposes that only by taking into account partial and mixed meanings will it be possible to elaborate future alternatives, since one hope has expired: that of unilinearly ciphering all desires for social liberation into a single kind of emancipatory protagonism from which change ensues, following a singular law of historic transformation.

All these revisions to the avant-garde model of art came into play informally in the redefinition of a new cultural sensibility that began operating in Chile after the 1980s. It was a sensibility defined by "an ebb in the heroic sense of art and literature (as 'consciousness raising'), a distancing from the model of the charismatic intellectual, as interpreter of the people and bearer of the meaning of history," by its "distance from artistic populism and cultural nationalism," and by the desire "to erase the traces of teleological thought and erode the traditional idea of the uniqueness of the subject as the source of signification," among other traits.[24]

CADA's works deployed all their artistic potency in the midst of these contextual fractures that were driving a reconceptualization of the relationships between art, politics, and society. CADA was the first historical example of a Chilean avant-garde art, a paradigm of the saturated commitment between *aesthetic experimentation* and *political radicalism*. But that paradigm was put together aesthetically just as its field of references and sociocritical applications was falling apart. It was a field that no longer could respond to the utopian fantasy of a project for global emancipation because its subject expressed a diversified and plural constellation of aspirations, refusals, struggles, and contradictions, no longer reducible to a univocal conception of history.

POSTSCRIPT: THE CITATION THAT
RE-CITES ITSELF

According to standard international art histories, "the lasting contribution of the avant-gardes—once they enter their state of historical fixity, that is, once their programmatic desire to fuse artistic practice with the exercise of life has been foreclosed—is the general availability of their techniques."[25] Seen from the limited inventory of Chilean art, in which techniques and productive media are more restrictive than expansive, the availability in question becomes more likely that of "a sum of gestures," as Pablo Oyarzún states. And in the case of the avanzada's art, this sum was in turn added—in an exemplary way—to the symbolism of the "gesture of the appropriation of art as the appropriation of one's 'own' history."[26] What became of that avant-garde gesture when it was revisited by one of its founding authors in Chile—at a time when history, signs, and institutions already had liberated themselves from their antagonistic past—in order to rearticulate new pacts of social understanding in the language of consensus?*

In August 1993 the Chilean poet Raúl Zurita effected an intervention in the Northern Chilean desert (fifty-six kilometers inland from Antofagasta) that consisted of inscribing on its surface a phrase three kilometers long: "Ni pena ni miedo" [Neither grief nor fear].† Zurita—an ex-founding member of CADA—enacted a double citation. He re-cited his own poetry that, since his 1979 collection *Purgatorio* [Purgatory], had used the trope of the Chilean desert to configure the evangelizing role of a "new writing" capable of transcending the pain of national crucifixion. And he cited—by inverting its supports—"Las escrituras en el cielo" [Sky Writing], which he had realized in 1982 with CADA in New York City.

Today's Zuritian gesture reiterates two of the neo–avant-garde postulates that CADA's works articulated: (1) that of dissolving the boundaries between traditional genres by effecting an action not framed within any established format (the work is "neither poetry, sculpture, painting, architecture, monument, 'public work,' publicity, nor popular maxim,"[27] while it simultaneously is all of these at once), and (2) that of displacing the creative gesture to a vital support (the Chilean landscape) where the work could be accessed by virtually anyone—in this case, any airborne passenger—without the cultural overdetermination of an artistic frame of reference. The work reissues CADA's transgeneric crossings, but without the aggressive anti-institutionality of a gesture that sought to fracture the artistic-literary system. By not being identified as generic conventions, these artistic supports become easily interchangeable: the work is "part of a poem that in an instant passes from one support to another,"[28] without intending to violate any system of cultural demarcation. The expansion of enunciative supports that Zurita's writing effects (from the page of a book to the Chilean desert) has, rather, the value of prolonging/continuing the *poetic dream* of imagining a world without material restrictions or practical limitations. If the poet can occupy the world as a book, it is because—romantically speaking—the imagination has no limits, at least within the tradition of metaphysical and religious idealism that, via the newspaper El Mercurio, consecrated the reading of Zurita's work in Chile.

But another critical tension of the neo–avant-garde citation also disappears in this more contemporary gesture: that which situated past, present, and future in a relationship of antagonisms and contradictions. The phrase "Neither grief nor fear" seeks, according to Germán Bravo, "to account for a historical experience, not only of a political break but of a break in the very possibility of communication and community . . . and it attempts to remove the lesson of that experience from the communicative capacity of Chilean society, in order to erect itself as a signal in the desert indicating the coordinates of what is possible after Hell." [29] The phrase "Neither grief nor fear" interprets the theme of memory in postdictatorship Chile: the traumatized memory of the past (pain, wound) that must be recuperated as history (scar) by a society already deeply invested in the hope of a tranquil future. The two time frames that the phrase conjoins speak to us about a past one need not lament and a future one need not fear: the conflictive character of both temporalities is neutralized here by a present that reconciles them. If we reconvert the ethical-political figure of national memory (the subject that the phrase's content evokes) to the languages of the avant-gardes (that give the evocation of this theme its artistic form), it appears that Zurita's phrase suppresses the conflicting relationship between past, present, and future, when it is precisely that conflict that serves to mobilize his neo–avant-garde gesture to intervene vehemently against the past (the heretical gesture of destruction) in favor of the future (the saving promise of a utopia yet to be realized). Past and future finally have been harmonized here by the mediation of a conciliatory present that tranquilizes and reconciles, that ponders and controls, those excesses of a historic temporality that the avant-garde will to rupture sought to disrupt. The present's moderation is the point of equilibrium that deactivates the antagonisms and contradictions between these two temporalities today happily reunited. The present is no longer experienced as a problem (obstacle, challenge), but rather as a solution benefitting from the help of intermediaries — "a secretary of state and various entrepreneurs" [30] —who contributed to the materialization of the artwork. That present, which deactivates the tension between present and future by coordinating both periods under a tranquilizing decree ("Neither grief nor fear"), is not the restless present of the avant-garde, but rather the quieted (calmed, satisfied) present of the institutional consecration of the "great work." This "great work's" calmness comes to it not only through "the sensation of concluding, of finishing a cycle."[31] It also comes from the sublime image of a present "suspended in the air" that *transcends* the earthly vicissitudes of the here and now, dehistoricizing itself: returning to the primeval vision of the desert's natural landscapes as a "place so absolutely free from contamination that it seems to be the second day of creation."[32] The desert in Zurita's phrase becomes a transit zone that joins humanity's past and times to come thanks to *myth* as the figure of repetition: "we can only turn in circles" between "times that have been repeating themselves for millennia and that will continue to repeat themselves,"[33] says Zurita. The biblical resonance of the desert's geography consecrates it as immemorial space. It is this *immemorial* quality of the desert that charges Zurita's phrase about *memory* with wisdom and transcendence. The Chilean avant-garde gesture of "appropriating one's 'own' history"—in the double sense of an individual (Zurita's work) and collective (the nation's) history—that Zurita re-cites is displaced here to the immaterial, *eternal present* of the desert's mythical language. This language is the *infinity* of representation: a language that flies over the present, lending itself to an allegorical reading from the sky as a hyperspace of continuous reception, without social demarcations or cultural punctuation. The symbolism of the sky as total space (without interruptions or disequilibria) thus sutures the gap between poetics and politics, thanks to the democratic transition's institutionality. Such institutionality *promotes* and *mediates* the fulfillment of the *utopian dream*, making it a *reality*, and nullifying it—pragmatically—as the desire to dream the impossible.

THREE

Destruction, Reconstruction, and Deconstruction

During the period of the military government, Chile split into two discursive fields that sought to reorganize themselves, under inverse signs, around their fracturing. The victimizing pole disguised its seizure of power as a foundational break and made violence (both brute and institutional) the instrument of a fanaticizing Order, operating as the disciplinary mold of an obligatory truth. The victimized pole traumatically learned to dispute the meanings of official discourse, achieving a rearticulation of dissident voices within alternative microcircuits that impugned the regulating format of a single signification.

The historical and political dramatization of this break [i.e., the imposition of military rule] as a *separation* between before and after, inside and outside, above and below, and so forth, reinforced an ideological polarization of cultural practices strictly governed by the ethical-political division between the *official field* (integrated into the military regime's double language of "modernization-repression") and the *unofficial field* (which rejected the dictatorial paradigm). The exaggerated division between these two, mutually incommunicative, camps forced each to give the appearance of an ostensible uniformity and internal coherence that never really existed, since both fields were traversed by the irregularities and contradictions of often uncoordinated conjunctural movements. The contestatory pole suffered especially from the reductionism of that uniform vision, prisoner of a dualism imposed by a negative polarity (the dictatorship) that rigidly overdetermined the entire range of antagonistic relationships.

Despite the fact that conflicts were often "more intense within the unofficial field than between it and the official field,"[1] there was always a tendency to overprotect the converging motivations uniting forces of the opposition by diverting analysis away from those points of ideological-cultural disagreement articulated by internal polemics. It is true that there were many reasons for disregarding the conflicts among languages that threatened to pull apart what had been so arduously drawn together in response to the antidictatorial call. It was not desirable to keep fragmenting a territoriality of voices already dislocated historically by so many violations of identity, or to weaken still further a plotting of solidarity already made sufficiently fragile by the adversity of the context. However, the points of ideological-cultural divergence apparent among practices in the opposition camp highlighted certain controversies of meaning that are particularly significant from the (tense and intense) point of view of a discussion about form and ideology, poetics and politics.

Bringing to light today this group of practices—including those previously silenced counterpositions and disagreements—provides a backdrop of greater critical density for analyzing the cultural transformations engendered during the past decade [the 1980s], as they anticipated the mutating sensibilities traversing the panorama of the democratic transition.

CULTURE AND THE LEFT(S)

The military coup presented itself as "a great ordering act," fraudulently associated with "the basic security of the individual, and with conceptions of purity and pollution, classification and identity, sin and pardon, guilt and shame, domination and production, the permissible and the taboo."[2] A first axiom of the discourse of authoritarian-totalitarian power consisted of a fanatical adherence to order as a classifying principle for discourses and identities. It is the dichotomizing rigidity of the separation between superior and inferior, exterior and interior, light and dark, pure and contaminated, and so forth, that categorically structures the mythical-political symbolism inspiring foundational discourses. To put in order and call to order are the routinizing slogans through which a regime of (brute and institutional) force feigns an appeal to constructive rationality, in order to disguise the arbitrary cuts of its destructive violence. This appeal reiterates, with each framing formula, the regime's role as guardian of a fixed repertoire of inalterable values. These values are to be defended, against the threat of disorder's specter as chaos, through purifying-decontaminating rites that expel the "other" (the dissimilar) from the semantic universe governed by the equation Order = Purity, guarantor of homogeneity and transparency.

During the military regime, the manic-obsessive reiteration of the call to Order was aimed at both *politics* (action) and the *political* (discourse) as manifestations of dis-order that transgressed the normative frame of the regime's self-founded—and unique, definitive—truths: truths closed in on themselves by a doctrinary chain that sought to reinforce the inexpungability of meaning.

The persecution and censorship of politics and the political during the first years of the military government led art and literature to serve as substitute means for the evocation-invocation of silenced voices.

As the repressive frame loosened and fissures opened within it, which the opposition could use to gain tactical mobility, contestatory culture progressively shifted from the semi-clandestinity of its first networks to circuits with greater public visibility. The sociocultural recomposition of these microcircuits, ever-growing in situational efficacy, gradually marked out a path between "*contestatory culture*" and "*alternative culture.*" It signaled the move from a culture conceived of as the mere prolongation of defeat, and as a rite of survival reaffirming what had been denied, to a culture capable of becoming the bearer of new forms and discursive styles pointing toward more complex differentiations of meaning. This move had as its correlate—after 1983*—the gradual repoliticization of diverse segments of social practice and the rearticulation of party politics for forces on the left. With this restoration of the most habitual channels of expression and political participation, art and culture began to return to their more specific—differentiated—fields of language and function. But even taking into account the progressive redelimitation of these fields in favor of greater autonomy for their respective discourses and practices, the left's ideological program still strongly connoted those cultural images mobilized by the antidictatorial front, up through the final struggles for regaining democracy.

The profound political convulsions unleashed by the dictatorial rupture, and the configuration of new social contexts that stimulated the disintegration of the old schema of ideological representation and partisan structures, led the Chilean left to face a large-scale crisis during the dictatorship years. This crisis, simultaneously historical-political and theoretical-programmatic, was accentuated by the international critical revision of historical Marxism and by the failure of "real socialisms." The positions adopted by the Chilean left in view both of these challenges and of the need for theoretical and political redefinition gradually took on "the bifurcated quality characterizing the dominant matrix of the Chilean left": toward a first tendency marked by "the classical Marxist-Leninist sectors of the left" and a second tendency influenced by "the sector of socialist renewal."[3] This division—between a classical or traditional left "manifested principally through the Communist Party, and secondarily through a segment of the Socialist Party and the MIR," and a renewal left "expressed in broad sectors of the Socialist Party and of the parties split from the Christian Democrats (MAPU, Christian Left, MAPU-OC)"[4]—not only identified two separate lines of thought and of sociopolitical conduct, but also constituted two types of reflection about aesthetics, culture, and politics.†

By then, culture did not possess the same valence of meaning for both lefts: it was neither conceived according to the same expectations nor expressed through networks of similar density. The traditional left continued to locate culture in a relationship of instrumental subordination to politics, as a "front for struggle" in the service of other correlated forces structuring that national juncture of partisan advancement. In the meantime, the renewal left critiqued the reductionism (both economic and political) of the traditional left and projected an anthropological-social vision of cul-

ture that privileged it as the much more diffuse space "of mediations, of struggles about meaning, of the construction of identities, the circulation of knowledge, the modeling of perception, in
short, of the social construction of reality."[5] The traditional left continued to elevate the working class as the only representative of revolutionary Truth and the "national-popular" as the anti-imperialist
symbol of what was Latin American. Meanwhile, the new left articulated its project of socialist renewal under the intellectual direction of the social sciences, citing work by authors of contemporary
international theory (Gramsci, Williams, Foucault, Bourdieu, etc.) in
order to critique Marxist-Leninist ideologism. While the traditional
left recurred to national calls and massive convocations organized
through grassroots cultural organizations, socialist renewal intellectuals employed the technical format of research for publishing their
theoretical-political analyses as material for international academic
discussion.

The most emblematic configuration of opposition culture was
always designed by the partisan regrouping of the traditional left—
from the first cultural coordinators to the actions in support of the
return to democracy, and passing through associations of artists and
writers' societies. The traditional left mobilized popular allegiances
to national themes, charged with symbolizing the collective forces
of energetic protest and militant conviction. The left of the "opposition cultural front" had begun privileging those ritualizing manifestations of a "we" rooted in communal traditions (folklore, popular music, etc.) that commemorated the past through symbolic acts
such as festivals or homages. Such manifestations recovered historical memory and reconstituted the nexuses of social existence, and
were directed toward a community anxious to share with a sacrifi-
cial Chile the ethos of its culture of martyrdom. Although many of
these manifestations entered into crisis when their expressive formats and organic-partisan frameworks became exhausted as the dictatorship wore on, the traditional left never stopped favoring a type
of culture "national in its roots" and "popular in its content,"[6] belonging to that "Latin American tradition that tends to identify 'left'
with 'popular.' "[7]

According to the militant culture's ideological-cultural sensibility, art above all should offer a testimony of rejection and denouncement. That is, it should fulfill the protest and consciousness-raising function of "narratives of urgency," whose subjects speak from the lived experiences of zones of exclusion and social repression, and serve as a depository for the ethical-symbolic truth of communal disintegration.

In 1977 the "avanzada" or "new scene" emerged with its neo–avant-garde bent, bringing together writers (Raúl Zurita, Diamela Eltit, Gonzalo Muñoz, etc.), artists (Eugenio Dittborn, Carlos Leppe, Carlos Altamirano, Lotty Rosenfeld, etc.), critics (Adriana Valdés, Eugenia Brito, etc.), and philosophers (Ronald Kay, Patricio Marchant, Pablo Oyarzún, etc.). The "new scene" brought together these voices around intense ruptures of languages whose *deconstructive* and *parodic* accent strongly clashed with the *emotive-referential* tone of militant culture. This "new scene" burst onto the cultural milieu with traits that made it "completely new due to its rigor, its critical level and the multiplicity of its linguistic operations, as well as its radical dismantling of the institutional notions of representation."[8] According to Gonzalo Muñoz, it eventually configured "a privileged moment of lucidity that returned Chilean art to its protagonistic place as an autonomous crafter of languages and as a center for producing new articulations of thought."[9]

"New scene" works also advocated the breakdown of the repressive system, but they did so using images and words as zones of symbolic fracturing in the official codes of cultural thought. While leftist culture's art of solidarity was received via transcendent humanistic readings that shared its faith in heroic feats, the "new scene" twisted alphabets in order to communicate its suspicion of those truths reabsolutized by militant dogma. The antilinear ruptures put into practice by the "new scene" strongly jolted the voluntary continuity of symbols through which the traditional left sought to politically reconnect a yet-to-be-constructed future with the destroyed past. After 1983, this continuity was endorsed by "the return of great figures from exile, who seemed to insert themselves almost naturally into the processes of rearticulation and redefinition of alliances among the leading groups opposing the regime, providing them with necessary faces for the visible configuration of a cultural front."[10] That front's answer to the threat represented by the new aesthetics' eruptive and disruptive cut was generally one of confining "the experimental adventure of the 'avanzada' to the volatile space of a parenthesis"[11] that did not obstruct the transcendent course of history—thanks to which the country was beginning to take ownership again of its social and political macronarrative. Even today, the "new scene" of art and literature of the 1980s still is viewed by the historian's gaze as an incidental and digressive episode, unconnected to the before and after of its emergence, an episode whose disconnectedness is such that it makes difficult the "new scene's" assimilation into those accounts of the period supported by the interpretive mechanics of linear processes.

The unsettling of the entire structure of collective representation —archived in memory and the past, ritualized in symbols, subjectivized in beliefs and imaginaries—that was unleashed by the 1973 coup could only provoke feelings of dispossession. The expropriating violence of the new strong-arm regime made many artists feel they should respond to the moral imperative of reconstituting a meaning fallen to pieces and thereby remedy the effects of the shattering of identity: patching up histories, reconfiguring totalities. From there followed the mystical solidarity of a "we" that could reconstitute shared life experiences, the restoration of traditions in images of the past that progressively reforged ties of belonging and communal grounding, the remythification of the "national-popular" as the absolute trait of a homogenous class and national consciousness, and the messianic fundamentalism of utopias.

While the culture of the traditional left reassigned transcendence to history as its redemptive resolution, the "new scene" played—in an antihistoricist way—with exploding signs in an ephemeral *poetics of the event*, "in the trenches of the discontinuous, of the partial, of lightning-fast actions."[12] That micropoetics of historical explosion and temporal discontinuity in art-situations, such as those put into practice by Lotty Rosenfeld and the group CADA in their video installations, was precisely what a painting of History like José Balmes's or Gracia Barrios's sought to *transcend* by "making visible the most ephemeral imperative and rendering it visible forever."[13] Such work held that "the continuity of this tracing is what comprises history; the continuity of an evanescent order, which for us is converted, from the moment of its installation, into a permanent memory."[14] Instead of suturing together the cuts, patching together versions of continuity and totality, "new scene" works elaborated "histories left unfinished" through "an accumulation of fragments that, distanced from their narratives, become interconnected in open possibilities, or deny their potential to become discourses."[15] Francisco Brugnoli stated this in defense of an *intermittent* and *discontinuous* memory, one that would not conceal the multiple pockets of meaning provoked by the unplotting of the codes of social and historical reference.

The subject postulated by the new aesthetics no longer coincided with the deep and true identity of humanistic morality, one that still maintained the integrity of the subject as a full and coherent foundation for representing the world. The subject of art and literature for the "new scene" was that "nonsubject, the subject in crisis, deconstructed, fragmented into multiple impulses,"[16] that expressed itself through personal biography in reaction to the failure of large ideological delineations of collective identity. Those diminished expressions of a fragile, trembling identity did not fit with the Subject of Resistance—trophy of the progressive ideary—that the culture of solidarity erected as the guarantor of a compensatory morality. The "new scene" knew that "what was previously the epic quality of acts and the certainty of meaning" was today only "the biographical remnant of a shattered history, the tattered testimony of a banner that still flies, but at half mast."[17] The only admissible possibility, then, was to structure a *counter-epic*, taking hold of intermediate, deemphasized registers, such as the domestic or urban domains, whose icons "are silent and indifferent, and whose flashes of meaning are opaque. They do not proclaim or challenge; they do not have medals to display or wounds to consider,"[18] in the words of the visual artist Carlos Altamirano. The subject of that counter-epic was divided into a schizoid

multiplicity of fractions of subjectivity open to the vertigo of disconnections, a subject wandering in the labyrinth of an "I" that "looks
for itself in continuous reflections, in repeated echoes, through different masks."[19] This subject surrendered to the "great mobility and
constant mistakes involved in this interplay of mirrors, settings,
makeup, and disguises," and its writing "integrated everyday violence into discourse itself, where it not only was explicitly mentioned
but also could be perceived in breaks, syntactic ruptures, phonetic
ambiguities, semantic play, and displacements of meaning: in the
unrefined speech of a voice whose pronouncements obeyed no rules
in changing grammatical persons, and in the sexual indeterminacy
of a continual movement from masculine to feminine."[20]

SIGNS, SYSTEMS OF POWER, AND CRITIQUES OF REPRESENTATION

The traits signaling the abrupt changes wrought by the "new scene"
in Chilean art and literature all converge on the ruptures generated
by its "inexhaustible activity for reformulating signs, an activity con-
tinuously permeated by critiques of representation, of artistic genres, of their underlying codes, of the languages of art."[21]

Undoubtedly one of the first reasons that the official left had for
distrusting the practices of the "new scene" stemmed from that de-
constructionism of signs in a permanent state of critical hyperactiv-
ity. And it also stemmed from the "cultural density" of the "new
scene's" plotting of "nonlocal referents (in general, and simplify-
ing, postmodernism)" and of "sublocal referents (such as those belonging to a culture of resistance or alternative culture),"[22] which
traversed quite dissimilar horizons of references and cultural experience. The difficulty of these crossings effectively overburdened acts
of reading with layers of opacity and excessive demands, presuppos-
ing a reader who was not only complicit but also expert in trans-
codifying maneuvers. The affectation of certain moves intended to
divert the course of official interpretations using strategically de-
ceptive meanings that would escape censorship, as well as the critical self-reflexivity of intertextuality and the play of quotations, to-

gether transformed the act of reading these works into an exercise of cryptoanalysis that challenged the presupposed transparency of direct forms of communication. All of these transversal operations exacerbated by the "new scene" were precisely what led the culture of the traditional left to reject it from its affective-effective circle, relegating it "to the margins, even of the unofficial field."[23]

The social and political marginalization of the "new scene" sanctioned the overflowing of practices located along the border zones of the sociocommunicative pact of the majority's shared culture. The *move-beyond-the-frame* (that is, breaking the canonical traditions' conventional formats) put into practice by the "new scene" metaphorized the will to transgress the concentration-based logic of spaces under surveillance, "generating other signals, plural symbols . . . to break the hegemonic outline of the frame itself,"[24] a frame as much territorial as ideological. The "new scene's" extramural and unintegrated narratives set loose a fugitive imaginary that gave mobility and itinerancy to the concept of *margin* as a figure enabling experiences with signs related to what Bakhtin called "the culture of limits."

Beyond the topographic fact of its location on the fringes of the system of power, the margin served as a concept-metaphor for rendering productive the social discarding of marginalization and marginality, converting its sanctioning into an *enunciative posture* and into the *aesthetic citation* of a critical neo-experimentality on the borders of identity and meaning. This concept-metaphor posed the critical tensionality of the boundary (artistic and biographical, gender-sexual) as a zone from which resonated questions of how territorial demarcations of symbolic power operate. It projected the model of a new type of social critique that sought to disorganize the rules for composing order and power from *within* (from the *in-between* of) its logics of symbolic and communicative functioning. And it was constructed in opposition to the political left's majority culture, which remained beholden to a model for critiquing the system based on a monolithic representation of power, governed by the image of a fixed centrality derived from the referent of the state. Realizing that "it was a question of politicizing art in the absence of orienting markers or solid directives,"[25] the "new scene" sought to elaborate *interstitial* tactics for subverting authoritative norms, multiplying small margins for the insubordination of signs within the system of repressive punctuation. In the words of Gonzalo Muñoz: "It was not only about eliding the rules of the game—itself always a reaffirmation of those rules—but rather about circumscribing them in their very senselessness. To expose them by driving them to their symbolic excess, to their limits. And to demonstrate at the same time a possible method for their deactivation."[26] A method that took aim at corporeality, sexual biography, the suburban plot and street aesthetics, everyday popular culture and feminine domesticity, as planes and sequences of life that should be interrupted and reformulated in an antiauthoritarian way. For the new aesthetics, it was precisely about overcoming that historical juncture's model of "a critique restricted to the authoritarian system,"[27] in order to transfer that critique to other discursive registers complexly implicated in the problematics of cultural domination and symbolic violence. The "new scene's" passion for dismantling meaning transformed its critique of *power in representation* (the official power's totalitarianism) into a critique of *representations of power*— that is, into a critique of figurations of the system that reiterated the violence of discursive intimidation in each enunciated series, grammatical chain, or subordinate phrase. This passage from one model of social critique to another proved decisive in setting the stage for negotiating the transition, that is, for gradually learning how to re-situate the strategies of cultural resistance in a much more plural and diversified field of forces than under authoritarianism. Having learned to disorganize the *subplot* of the categories and representations of symbolic power, the "new scene" was prepared to face the challenge of reimagining—in a postdictatorship landscape—forms of critiquing institutional culture that could be as *transversal* as possible.

This critique of the multiple compositions of power socially knotted together took off in various directions, leading to a complex reflection about marginalities and subalternities. It was a reflection about the play of positions and territorial operations set up around power (hierarchies, subordination, margins, segregation, boundaries, disseminations, etc.), combining—in an emancipatory way—

the categories of *feminine* and *Latin American* within a paradigm of the counterhegemonic. Such a combination—given shape publicly by the national relevance of the first "International Conference on Latin American Women's Literature" organized entirely by women in August 1987[28]—brought together the critical potential of the most reflexive forces deployed by the aesthetics of the periphery and the figures of alterity and decentering. Figures that interwove themes such as the rupture of the unitary subject as the matrix of universal representation, the dispersion of meanings as resistance to the dominant control of a monologic interpretation of culture, and the heterogeneity of bodies and voices not subjected to the canon of the origin's and the center's founding authority. These are the themes, elaborated multidirectionally, that "connected with theories of postmodernity" and produced the unusual precedent that "the incorporation of debate about this phenomenon (postmodernity)— which in the countries of the center took place simultaneously in philosophy, art and cultural history, the social sciences, and in art practices and criticism—took place, by contrast, in the Chilean case, almost exclusively through the artists of the 'new scene.' "[29]

FOUR

The Social Sciences:

Front Lines and Points of Retreat

The frequently uneasy and conflicted relationship between sociological discourse and aesthetic-critical thought seems to confirm Pierre Bourdieu's opinion that "sociology and art do not make good bedfellows."[1] Bourdieu explains their misencounters as resulting primarily from the clashing of two incompatible perspectives on art: the idealism of a sacred vision of art (transcendence, mystery, solitude, inspiration, etc.) predominates among artists, while among sociologists prevails a scientific rationalism, one that seeks to translate—and reduce—the artists' belief in the "immateriality" of art to the functionalism of statistical data. But this explanation cannot adequately account for the more complex disagreements that continue to oppose aesthetics and sociology, even in cases in which both disciplines have critically revised and overcome the ideological and cultural assumptions behind their core misunderstanding. On the contrary, these disagreements become more acute when sociology faces an art that has abandoned the idea of existing passively for collection and contemplation, to become instead a *poetics of disorder* whose convulsions of signs threaten to upset the hierarchy of social thought's established knowledge systems.

I would like to reinterpret these misencounters between artistic-cultural production and sociological theory by anchoring myself in a locally situated analysis that refers back to the specific circumstances of Chilean cultural debate over the last decade [the mid-1980s through the early 1990s]. On the one hand, the academic prestige of the Chilean social sciences (achieved by such renowned authors as José Joaquín Brunner, Norbert Lechner, etc.), and on the other, the complexity and audacity of the socio-aesthetic reformulations elaborated by the *nueva escena* ("new scene") in Chile during the same years in which the social sciences developed their theories about authoritarianism and redemocratization, can help us flesh out, in an exemplary way, the meaning of such misencounters. Their meaning is not solely relevant for one historical juncture. Rather, it suggests a *critical tension* between regular and irregular knowledge systems, between techniques of defense and audacious languages, between forces of demonstrative proof and zones of experimentation, between disciplinary contentions and the overflowing of genres.

THE NEW SCENE
OF CRITICAL THOUGHT

Repressive violence and ideological censorship during the dictatorship in Chile decisively altered those conditions for the production and dissemination of knowledge that, until 1973, had been guaranteed by the academic prestige of the Chilean university circuit. This was a circuit that, in the sixties, instituted a paradigm of intellectual life inspired by the image of the thinker as an agent of social and political change, mobilized by revolutionary utopianism. With the military intervention, the university lost its national leadership role in channeling the flow of ideas, while outside its walls, an explosive surging of what Rodrigo Cánovas called a "discourse of the crisis"[2] took place. This was a discourse that confronted the lively exteriority (beyond the walls) of processes and events denied by the university's closure: a discourse that set loose a kind of writing whose necessary and urgent combativeness demanded liberation from the technicalities of academic knowledge systems as well as overcoming the expository neutrality of scientific meta-languages. Starting in 1977, that discourse—"which took on its militant expression among a group of artists and their adherents in certain philosophical and literary circles"[3]—accompanied an art practice intent on formally dismantling the artistic and literary ideologies of cultural tradition. In close proximity to operations destined to underscore the materiality of the visual or textual signifier as a point of departure and process for the critique of the signified, this new discourse progressively explored zones of thought that manifested a desire for *experimentation with meaning* more than for *interpretation of meaning.*

This new "discourse of the crisis" circulated as "the informal theoretical referent in which were expressed those transdisciplinary directions that academic institutionality omits or relegates to its inner margins: Benjamin, psychoanalysis, semiotics, poststructuralism, and deconstruction."[4]

But neither Benjamin nor Freud nor Nietzsche nor Derrida entered into the functional apparatus of texts as fetishized citations of the metropolitan culture's philosophical knowledge system. Instead, they appeared as pieces to reassemble, connected to the psychosocial strata of the Chilean body, and mobilizing signifying energies through various conjunctions and collisions of references and experiences. The heterodox theorizations of the "discourse of the crisis" stressed the transdisciplinarity of boundaries of thought, disregarding the marks of established knowledge systems. Their movement beyond the stockpiles of knowledge protected by disciplinary legacies violated the cult of specialization in academic culture and questioned its legitimating hierarchies.

Texts of the new Chilean discourse assembled and disassembled knowledge systems with the help of the *citation*—and its quality of "cutting in." Similarly to how it was used in the art and literature of the same period, the citation became the technique that resignified —in an interrupted and discontinuous way—a culture and society *in pieces.* It allowed the recycling of origins and filiations into a mixture of intertextual sources and destinations, revealing the cultural transfer of languages on loan. The citation also staged a *montage* of meaning (associations/disassociations, combinations) without concealing any of its rough discontinuities, at a time of sociohistorical fracturing and breaks. Rather, the citation *effected a gash* so that what was enunciated could make *palpable* the wounds inflicted on knowledge systems by the destructuring of frameworks of experience and understanding within the Chilean universe. While official culture spoke the language of totalitarian rationality, of the repressive closure's indestructible Totality, the citation traced fissures and rents in the face of that Totality, destroying [des-trozando] its whole truths and multiplying the fragments [trozos] that an active thought process recombined as a jumble of parts and meanings. The juxtaposition of citations comprised a collage/montage technique that the texts employed to break the forced linearity of meaning, programmed in an authoritarian manner through false images of enunciative coherence. Heterogeneity and dissemination were the marks that revealed a meaning "open to contingency, broken at its joints" (Oyarzún), thanks to those citations that reintroduced in the interior of the enunciation all the contradictions that unsettled and destabilized the presupposition of formal harmony. With this rearrangement of enunciations, the texts' orientation recalled convulsions in their surroundings, rendering more acute—through cuts and additions—the brute materiality of the rubs and friction between corpus and surface, and provoking a collision of irruptive and disruptive forces whose tremors negated the possibility of calmly plunging into the interiority of meaning.

Chilean readers of the "discourse of the crisis" passed through that field of citations as through a zone of convergences and intersections of mutilated knowledge systems and disciplines fractured by the un-disciplining of genres. In that zone, the amalgamation of "life and (artistic and theoretical) work" interpellated readers provocatively from a position of "transgression and (sexual, linguistic, and symbolic) marginality."[5] These fields of citations and zones of collisions assaulted that discourse of the measurable and calculable professed—in the same years—by the social sciences. The social sciences had sought to maintain *control of meaning* based on rules of objective demonstration or proof and on the technical realism of an efficient knowledge system refunctionalized for a scientific/financial market that would determine its international acceptance. A market that had "its technical support in the word processor" and that triumphantly put forth the *paper* as "the letter of introduction" conveying "a new pragmatism entrenched in a language for undermining all critical and fictionalizing aspects in favor of their serial and abstract manipulation."[6]

DETOURS AND DEVIATIONS

The "new scene's" practices, restricted to minority audiences, "consciously shifted toward the margins of culture, including those of alternative culture, in order to locate its search there, on the outer edges of communication and personal experience."[7] By contrast, the "unofficial [social sciences], excommunicated, expelled from the universities,"[8] while also forming part of the alternative movement, "sought to reconnect with public opinion and the mechanisms of intellectual influence—magazines, academies, public fora, embassies, political parties, prestigious international and local networks."[9] These disparities of support and organization account for the unequal positions of each sector on the map of sociocultural recomposition. But they do not completely explain why the relationships of theoretical and critical exchange between the social sciences and the "new scene" were—in the words of Brunner himself —"varied according to each case and moment, but always tenuous, even reticent."[10]

The sector of social sciences grouped around FLACSO [Latin American Faculty of Social Sciences] in Chile was distinguished by its efficient recuperation of the site of academic prestige that had corresponded nationally to the intellectual enterprise of developing mediums for rationally analyzing the social and political realms. But it also was characterized by the remodeling of a new theoretical sensibility that strongly contrasted with the functionalist and Marxist tendencies that until then had dominated the institutional tradition of Latin American social sciences. This new sensibility emerged from changes marked by "doubts cast upon the great modernizing projects, which had constituted the basic substance of symbolic-political consumption in other times (whether development theory, liberalism, or socialism)" and by "the disenchantment and distrust generated by institutional ruptures, political failures, and social dismemberment."[11] Martín Hopenhayn calls this new current of sensibility "critical humanism," emphasizing with this designation Chilean sociology's particular way of combining contemporary culture's different systems of knowledge—sociological, theoretical, philosophical, and so forth. Chilean sociology used this combination of multiple and crossing knowledge systems to question the totalizing rationales of macrosocial schemes and to revalorize the local and everyday microdimensions of culture as a symbolic project for forming memory, constituting identities, and representing subjects through communicative interactions.

The theoretical and critical changes manifested by this new sensibility traversing Chilean social scientific thinking signaled that its authors shared with the artistic and cultural "new scene" a kindred frame of reference (namely, to simplify: post-Marxism in the social sciences, poststructuralism in artistic and literary theory) and that these convergent readings could have fed some type of complicit dialogue about a shared horizon of theoretical and cultural reconceptualization. This did not take place, however. Despite the fact that the theoretically renewed sector of the social sciences headed by José Joaquín Brunner demonstrated a greater perceptiveness and receptivity to the socio-aesthetic reformulations of the "new scene,"[12] a broader dialogue of productive communication between both sectors did not follow. Instead, mutual distrust and suspicion prevailed.

The centers of study spearheading analysis of the unofficial cultural field during the dictatorship (taking CENECA as a model)[13] chose to focus on cultural manifestations with a mass scope and distribution, whose sense of purpose—rooted in the popular—was communal reintegration. That research necessarily marginalized from its investigative purview the "new scene's" rupturistic breaks, stigmatized as a minority expression. Seen from the perspective prioritizing a commitment to social action or mass participation, the "new scene" seemed to be "a ghetto experience, distanced from the general evolution of the field, overdetermined by the conviction of its own values . . . with sectarian tendencies, indifferent to its audiences, with scant institutionalization, etc."[14]

On the one hand, the sociology of culture reproached the "new scene" for its vindication of the margin as a nonplace that excluded it (the "new scene") from the game of institutional and market reorganization beginning to energize—following the rhetoric of modernization—certain regions of the cultural landscape under authoritarianism. According to sociologists, the " 'new scene's' relationship of exteriority to (and rejection of) the market, repression, and television"[15] prevented it "from finding a venue to new audiences" that might break through the barriers of its self-absorption.[16] On the other hand, artists and critics reproached sociology's tendency to evaluate works according to mere "quantitative criteria of reception or of the massive scope of their production and distribution."[17] They accused sociology's "corrupt gaze" (Muñoz) of being complicit with isolating the most innovative practices of the period, leveling against it the very same complaints regarding the esoteric nature of its languages as those pronounced—in the name of common sense—by defenders of the *doxa*. A gaze that, "beneath the mask of functional sociologism, reproduced the logic of domination"[18] by labeling as *deviant* any gesture transgressing the norm of functional integration into the system of artistic consumption, without valorizing its oblique, *deviating* capacity: the critical twisting of the linearity of the dominant model of communication, namely, market- and industry-based cultural stereotypes. From the "new scene's" point of view, the social sciences' ability to go beyond a predetermined standard of social outcomes and performance failed. Such a standard measured the efficacy of artistic practices by verifying their results within the meager limits of numerical proofs fixed by the quantitative logic of its system: a logic based on "the capitalizing of cultural production" according to which "the work of art is merchandise" regulated by "the rationality of the market and of commercial circuits."[19] There remained lacking a willingness to risk valorizing the critical gesture of intervening and contravening the rules of adaptation to artistic conventions, starting with a breach open toward the more obfuscated zones of symbolic experience within Chile under the repression. Such a critical valorization would have contributed to the "new scene's" being "recognized by those significant audiences that transmit—toward the intellectual and artistic field, toward the press and

the professions, toward the middle sectors in intellectual occupa-
tions—a valorization of avant-garde or 'avanzada' works."[20] As
Brunner himself stated, "the initial recognition of the avant-garde
is hardly ever a phenomenon of consumption or acceptance by mass
culture," but rather depends on a "phenomenon of circulation
among audiences distinguished by their 'valorizing' position in the
cultural field."[21] Only the social sciences could have played that "valorizing" role adequately, thereby extending the limits of the debate
about neo–avant-garde and post–avant-garde criticism, about aesthetic ruptures and the cultural market, that "new scene" practices
had generated with such unusual vigor.

THE SOCIAL SCIENTIFIC GAZE
AND ITS BLIND SPOTS

The "new scene's" insurgent gestures operated "based on dispersion, on impulses, on the annihilation of unity."[22] By contrast, the
social sciences had to meet the requirements of a discourse financed
by international agencies that expected useful observations regarding
the social and political dynamics of processes necessarily implicated
in the reconstitution of subjects, since they were preparing the stage
for the protagonists of the democratic transition. It was a discourse,
then, that could only marginalize from the purview of its prepaid
research the analysis of twists and turns of identity and language
that the "new scene" practiced as excess: that is, as a nonutilitarian
marker of the squandering of figurative possibilities (allegories and
metaphors) that perturbed the precalculated economy of instrumental rationality. The "new scene's" gesture of "achieving a trembling
of aestheticized events" (Muñoz) exceeded the explanatory logic of
a functional sociologism that sought to account for what exploded
in the works as the "production, multiplication, and unfolding of a
symptom."[23]

   The sociological will to order categories and to categorize disorder—
to reframe the crisis of meaning in a secure language and a general
framework that could in turn discipline the meaning of the crisis—
was made more difficult given so much destructuring of codes. This

general framework was composed and imposed because there was no "other scheme produced by the Chilean intelligentsia of comparable validity, a comparable set of influences, or similar range of topics and problems."[24] But its necessarily totalizing character—its will to breadth and synthesis—also meant *realigning* what was *antilinear*: subjecting the twists and turns of tropes compelled by speech in crisis to the restructuring directionality of scientific rationality. This realignment obeyed "a particular, implicit understanding of the historical, as conceived from the social matrix, which is in turn viewed as an outgrowth of the political matrix."[25] It sought to channel the aesthetic flow of the "new scene" via a political and cultural rationalization that ended up silencing its most innovative countercurrents.

FLACSO and CENECA established themselves throughout Latin America as the centers for sociological investigation that effected the most extensive review of cultural phenomena in countries subjected to authoritarian control. But the accounting and recounting derived from those reviews tell us that "the version of our history that the social sciences offer speaks to us not only about that history, but also—and perhaps most of all—about the social sciences themselves, about the urgency of their own recomposition, their will to preserve and redefine the place of dominance in national discourse they had achieved beginning in the sixties,"[26] which had been disarticulated by the military coup. The Chilean social sciences exercised that dominance by describing and explaining a series of lived processes under the dictatorship, confidently supported by a "sociological paradigm for the analysis of culture offering a *macrosocial* characterization of modern forms of production, communication, and consumption, which in turn reach mass audiences and are achieved in accordance with the laws of the market."[27] This is the paradigm the "new scene" destabilized when it opened points of retreat and clandestinity in that framework of technical hyperrationalizations, when it inundated the regulatory cues of scientific abstraction with a turbulence of meaning.

The tensions produced between sociology's macrorationalizations and the "new scene's" narrative-visual micropoetics possessed critical traits that anticipated the cultural debate about modernity and postmodernity. Sociology "imagined itself as the privileged child of reason and attempted to organize the world according to the rationality of philosophers, from Comte to Marx,"[28] installed by Western modernity as the foundation of order and guarantee for understanding man and society. The breakdown of the paradigms of history (development, evolution, progress, etc.) that forced the critical redefinition of categories made universal by that same modernity from which sociology was born, together with the postmodern critique of the absolute rationality of omni-comprehensive systems, forced social theory to question its new conditions of knowledge production in the midst of so many blurred signals, crossed clues, and slippery accounts. This questioning, together with the historical experiences of dictatorship (authoritarianism and totalitarianism) and democratic reconstruction (diversity and plurality), led the Chilean social sciences to reorient their knowledge systems toward theoretical projects more sensitive to topics concerning "the social imaginary, the symbolic order, the languages of communication, everyday life, emergent or discarded utopias, new forms of urban sensibility or the rupture of dominant rationalities."[29] This change in repertoire was motivated by the ("postmodern") distrust of the systematizing macronarratives of social theory, a distrust shared entirely by the "new scene," which already had made this explicit through a micropoetics of fragmented identities and meanings. But the Chilean social sciences needed to make trustworthy the account of their distrust, inscribing it within the field of knowledge and acknowledgment accredited by the academic-professional lexicon's rules of validity and competence, while art and literature manifested their critique of totalizing rationality through the strategic placement of border subjects and objects, far from the hegemonies of knowledge stamped by diplomas of disciplinary obedience.

What those very same social scientists portrayed as one of the determining positions of the "new scene" in the eighties—that is, its "inexhaustible activity of reformulating signs, continually permeated by the critique of representation"[30]—was not limited to dismantling the ideological stereotypes of the contestatory testimonial genre. Rather, its passion for critical dismantling exceeded, in multiple directions and meanings, the conjunctural limit of the referent Dictatorship. The minimalism of syntactic breaks and fragments, opposing the epic of metasignification, assembled a stage of disassembly on which vocabularies in miniature signaled the downfall of global significations, the failure of totalizing abstractions, the disorientation and deflection of general perspectives based on fixed points or straight lines. These indicators of reformed thinking were traced by theoretical and cultural combinations that anticipated the turns of postmodern thought (heterogeneity, fragmentation, decentering, alterity, plurality, etc.) that the social sciences are beginning to consider today. In not paying sufficient attention to these combinations, the social sciences failed to take advantage of the critical potential of the scene that offered "the antecedent to the current discussion about postmodernity."[31] This scene had made evident how "art *experienced before* any other discipline in Chile (social and political sciences) the fall of the utopian subject and the discovery of the fragmentary and heterodox character of everyday experience"[32]—topics that later, in response to the crisis of political rationalities, would have to be incorporated into the cultural debate about democratic socialism.

The Chilean social sciences are at the forefront of efforts to revise those themes that had underpinned their intellectual enterprise (modernization, development, etc.) and won its fame. They are taking the lead, as well, in proposing retrospective and introspective readings of Latin American modernity (Brunner) as residual, decentered, anomalous, and so on, which have engaged the most suggestive themes to emerge from the postmodern critique of the uniform rationalities of the center's modernity. But when they found themselves faced with the "new scene's" *stylistic operations*, detached—critically and parodically—from the languages of modernity, these very same social sciences opted to protect themselves from such an adventure by taking shelter behind the screen—almost unchanged— of a "quantitative methodology" tracing "a statistical outline of the global development" of cultural transformation.[33] Despite their formal challenge to the totalizing abstractions of scientific practices linked to modern rationality, the social sciences left almost no room for "unsystematic observations regarding the meanings that processes have for subjects," which could defy "the interpretations constructed in macroanalyses" and thus renovate the conditions for reading determined by that globalizing framework.[34] They tended instead to relegate extrasystematic readings to the margins of their classified knowledge systems. Despite their having theorized Latin American modernity as a mixture and jumble of codes, multistratified by intercultural hybridization, "the hypotheses and lines of argument that they developed" were based on "the quantitative grasping of modernization's prevalent tendencies."[35] They did not permit more *nomadic* ways of knowing to cross-fertilize in a transdisciplinary manner, or to open spaces of legibility *between* disciplines, beyond the technical repertoires made conventional by the market of specializations.

It is because of all this that the Chilean sociology of the eighties could "appear modern, too modern" from the perspective of the "new scene," which carried out—in defiance—"a critique of modernity's key elements, such as the rejection of reducing truth to a group in power, including intellectuals recognized by some institutional mechanism; distrust of the power of analytical reasoning; rupture in the face of discursive language's pretensions; critique of the merely denotative and of any particular discipline's specialized lexicon."[36]

The semiperipheral operations of the "new scene"—which projected "an oblique gesture toward a certain economy, the illogical shadow of a certain dominant logic" (Muñoz)—deployed productive conditions for revising the monopoly of readings exercised by the social sciences, whose hegemonic tradition dominates Latin American cultural thought. This need for revision and critique grew out of the conflict between reasoning based on proof and pertinence and the irrationality of im-pertinent languages charged with an expressiveness that rebelled against the normativity of both frame and framework. These were languages that experienced new constructions of meaning appealing to forms of knowledge *outside the usual contracts*, and violating the habits of an academic culture that administers privilege, while leaving in the shadows of its legitimated knowledge the unguaranteed practices of more informal ways of knowing. That critique of the economy of intellectual power, based on a severing of specialization and professionalization, was achieved through the dispersed energies and creativity of a form of knowledge that was not institutionally recognized, but that was nevertheless capable of modulating changes in cultural and ideological sensibility after the dictatorship, and well before these shifts were expressed by social theory's repertoire of constituted and instituted forms of knowledge.

FIVE

Staging Democracy
and the Politics of Difference

The shift from politics as *antagonism* (the dramatization of conflict, as governed by the struggle against the dictatorship) to politics as *transaction* (a democracy of agreements, with its formula of pacts and technicized negotiation) could only bring paradoxes and dissonance. As Garretón, Sosnowski, and Subercaseaux state: "In the processes of democratization, once binding ties were broken and the negative project of the dictatorship versus culture was shattered, and once creative freedom of expression was established, it appeared we were living a new paradox. The energies that had been expressed in the cultural world, and that had contributed to setting in motion the democratization process, seemed to exhaust themselves and become submerged in the reborn world of politics, where everything is negotiation, arranged agreements [*concertación*],* a search for consensus, and the attenuation of cultural debate, in order to avoid any risk (real or imaginary) of a return to authoritarianism."[1]

How were such paradoxes formulated in the Chilean cultural milieu of the democratic transition, and how did they affect the renovation of its languages, as well as the rearticulation of its cultural forces and of its critical energies?

THE PLAY OF CULTURAL SYMBOLIZATION

Artists and intellectuals habitually complain that culture is always the object of marginalization and postponement, as compared to the priority of majority demands (like education, justice, work, health, etc.) on the calendar of issues determined by the national agenda. And it is true that culture is always at the mercy of *leftover* resources, because culture itself is conceptualized by political rationality as *excessive*, as a *surplus* of meaning. Art and literature's metaphors always speak to us of excess and immoderation, by overloading the practical-communicative content of messages regulating social interchange with *indirect forms*. Politics tends to protect itself from the ambiguity of signs with which cultural metaphors play, instead making culture functional and converting it into a mere *product* to be administered via regulatory apparatuses and bureaucratic coordination. In fact, this instrumental functionalism punishes the ways in which artistic and literary metaphors misspend the communicative budget of practical language (by adorning it with sumptuous and sumptuary arabesques of signs), and the ways in which such metaphors—driven by forms that act as accessories in the task of expressing art's commitment to a truth to be transmitted—betray a representational notion of the artistic message.

In order to imagine new relationships between culture and politics, it is first necessary to break the mechanistic paradigm signaling a causal determination between the social-real (productive rationality) and the cultural-ideological (symbolic expressivity). That paradigm only represses the autonomy-heteronomy of forms, by supposing that art and literature should be responsible solely for reflecting the conflicts already formulated and consigned by social rationality. As if culture were a mere expressive supplement-complement that, while retaining the privilege of transfiguring reality into symbols, lacks sufficient protagonism to critique the discursive organization of reality using models of alternative significations. To valorize such protagonism would imply recognizing culture's capacity to transform and rearticulate social determinants via the crossed interplay of counterresponses that exacerbate *asymmetries* and *disjunctures* to the point of breaking with the uniformity of serialized programmings outlined by the dominant rationality. The structural relationship between aesthetics and society is based not on the linear correspondence of form and content, but rather on responses set loose by the multiple fractures of signs involved in symbolic creation, which unsettle every order based on linear transfers between text and context. Culture does not illustrate social tensions as if they were the prefabricated referent that the work should passively reflect. What artistic-cultural practices do is actively dismantle and reformulate tensions and antagonisms via figurative languages that intervene in social discursivity, redistributing its signs, and changing them into new, multiple, and fluctuating constellations. It is then that these artistic-cultural practices mock ideology's zeal for unifying totalization. It is then that these practices show their capacity "to transcribe an articulated body of thought, but also its *vacillations* and *weaknesses*, the most obscure zones in which ideology gestates, bringing together conflicts and contradictions in its task of interpreting a concrete reality" through that which leaves behind *residues*.[2] As Angel Rama pointed out, it is then that "the multiplicity of levels and planes on which a work simultaneously develops" forms a "composed product, in which remain, with diverse intensity and depth, traces of their various sources, along with those of the concrete functioning of the field of forces" that the work displaced and reconfigured in designs alternative to those established by dominant codes.[3]

Revalorizing culture from a democratic point of view implies empowering it as the stage for symbolic-institutional mediations, where codes and identities interactively plot significations, values, and forms of power. A stage where the registers that articulate meaning are formed, and where meanings battle with the multiple conflicts of legitimacy and interpretation that enliven the debate of forms. This revalorization of culture as a *theater of representations* requires that we think about "the mechanisms of figurative language, of fiction, and of artifice," insofar as "they can help us to elaborate sharper constructions with regard to society, itself also composed, in great measure, of elusive desires, mirrors, shadows, and masks."[4] These shadows and masks make social science researchers realize they cannot keep ignoring that "there are basic questions that can be more subtly and effectively formulated if they are also conceived as ensembles of fictional maneuvers," associated with "the revealing potential of tropes that, on the one hand, disguise, obscure, and falsify, in order, on the other, to intensify significations and suggest new paths to comprehension."[5]

Taking into account the demobilizing crisis of paradigms affecting citizenship on the "post" horizon (leitmotif for any fin de siècle commentary about the weakening of ideologies and the failure of utopias), it is difficult to believe that politics will be able to recapture the social imagination without venturing into the "*rodeos y merodeos*" (Escobar) — into the roundabout and marauding aspects — of cultural symbolization. Such are the symbolizations that convince us, in García Canclini's words, that "perhaps the greatest interest for politics in taking into account the symbolic problematic lies not in the sure efficacy of certain goals or messages, but in the fact that the theatrical and ritual aspects of the social make evident what there is of the oblique, the simulated, and the deferred in any interaction."[6] Such are the symbolic performances plotted by the *figurativity* of cultural messages that recreate a density of events and meaning capable of reintensifying the matter of signs, today evacuated, for the most part, by the instrumental technicism of *data*.

REDEFINITIONS OF THE INTELLECTUAL

The democratic reaperture normalized the conditions of production and of sociocultural communication by revitalizing formats for public intervention (the press, television, the universities, government ministries, etc.) that the authoritarian regime's censorship had prohibited or restricted. This normalization of practices removed the drama from the relationships between culture and politics, which the dialectic of confrontation under the dictatorship had made static.

The new context — in which institutions shifted from authoritarian to conciliatory, from repressive to dialogue-based — made obsolete the rigid figure of radical exteriority, which had been the model of opposition to the system during the previous period, when the integrated and the marginal were regulated by a severe topography of inside/outside. This institutional reordering of the range of relationships between culture and politics led artists and intellectuals to revise their imaginary of rupture, previously tied to an oppositional culture that extracted its pathos from contestatory negativity. For those who resolved not to submit to the negotiating maneuvers of the administrative readjustment, the challenge of reelaborating new tactics for institutional critique meant learning a "trajectory that would go from rigid, fixed gestures to mobile, astute gestures."[7] A trajectory that prolonged the lessons the "new scene" learned along the way during the previous decade [the 1980s], by "engaging a space that did not respond to preconceived outlines" and "proposing an exploration of meaning, a perception of the experience of authoritarianism by means other than those then offered by ideological discourse."[8]

All of these changes in format and conduct again posed necessary questions regarding the work of artists, critics, and intellectuals—today inserted within the institutional apparatus of the democratic transition and placed in the service of legitimizing the consensus—regarding their capacity to continue formulating "opinions that disturb, impugn, interrogate, and open the horizon" of those meanings agreed upon and accepted by the majority.[9]

The most emblematic definitions of the intellectual in Latin America had been those traditionally forged by leftist thought. Such thought valorized intellectuals as producers or articulators of ideologies, who placed their capacity for rationalizing-synthesizing ideas and ideals in the service of the program of social struggle and political confrontation modeled by the revolutionary instrument of the political party. It was the intellectual who communicated a "worldview" assured by the certainty of holding the keys to the intelligibility of history and of being charged with communicating them as universal truth to the rest of society. It was the intellectual who spoke in representation-delegation of the class interests of the dispossessed and alienated sectors (the people, the masses), anticipating and mobilizing their collective coming to consciousness about the ultimate meaning of the battles of history. The Gramscian focus on the "organic intellectual" corrected that program of the Revolutionary Vanguard, by resituating the relationships between the intellectual class, various social sectors, and political parties within a more plural and stratified configuration of power struggles and competition for hegemony. Gramsci's conception of the organic intellectual as a "representative of hegemony" in turn was revisited through Foucault's new model of the "specific intellectual": intellectuals who *situate* their critique of power in the interior of the disperse multiplicity of its networks of enunciation and circulation, seeking to make them explode via oblique tactics of *local* resistance to the system's hierarchies. These successive redefinitions of the intellectual mark diverse types of relationships between theory and practice, knowledge and activism, criticism and ideology. And these relationships in turn involve diverse versions of how to articulate the nexus between the closed borders of culture as a specialized practice and the open field of social intervention. If, on the one hand, "the romantic idea of organic continuity between culture, ideology, and politics produces frequently undesirable linkages," on the other hand, "the affirmation of a radical autonomy between them hinders grasp[ing] the formal and conceptual complexity of each one."[10] Eluding the reductionism of such an opposition implies, in Beatriz Sarlo's words, "rethinking the relationship between culture, ideology, and politics as a relationship governed by a tension that cannot be eliminated, since this tension is the key to cultural dynamics. Thus, culture and politics can be considered nonsymmetrical and nonhomological."[11] It also implies conceptualizing these relationships not as invariable, "but rather [as] a product of cultural forms and the functions of ideology and politics in specific moments of a given society,"[12] and therefore as exposed to inevitable adjustments and reconversions.

What adjustments and reconversions mark the situation of the intellectual in Chile today?

It is necessary to signal right away that the precariousness of the Chilean cultural milieu does not permit the figure of the intellectual to be instituted as publicly as in other Latin American contexts, where intellectuals play a preponderant role in constituting national cultural thought. But, although carried out informally, certain public activities cast as intellectuals those who occupy important positions in some segment of the sociocultural panorama, symbolizing the prestige of their authority in public opinion. This is particularly the case of social scientists who, after having engaged under the dictatorship in theoretical-political reflection about the Chilean re-democratization process, find themselves incorporated today into the business of the democratic transition government's ministries. Legitimated as experts by the institutional machine of government politics, renowned economists and sociologists today display the planning-based rationality of their knowledge as a technical guarantee of efficiency. This rationality makes for a situation in which, "just as intellectuals used to dedicate themselves to converting theory into ideology, now those connected to power translate theory into measures."[13] The current order's imperative to plan requires thinking to be translatable and knowledge to be organized in terms of services and results: what, then, are the leftover margins within which those intellectuals might deploy themes that are *nonfunctional* for the administration of the current order?

This institutionalization of the intellectual function in times governed by the normalizing imperative of the recuperation-consolidation of order reopens the question—already formulated in other Latin American contexts of redemocratization—of how to learn to regularize the mechanisms of democratic consensus without that consensus generating only consent, thereby making "uneasiness stagnate within the habits of the institution, and making the intellectual a mere interpreter of order."[14] Carlos Altamirano continues: "For modernity not to be only a culture of efficiency and instrumental rationality, for democracy not to be only the preservation of the state of law and the ritualization of political competition, there will always appear, beyond those in power and those who aspire to power, beyond academic or state institutionalization, intellectuals who ask impertinent questions, reinterpret the struggle, make it appear, and legitimate issues that do not figure into the public agenda or merit the attention of the media."[15]

These impertinent questions that rebel against excessive institutional disciplining (against its overly normative systems of knowledge, its overly orthodox rationality) are the only ones charged with a critical energy that can correct the melancholic impression of those who feel, along with José Joaquín Brunner, that "with the passage of time, their conversations about culture" have become "each day something more like an exchange between government functionaries,"[16] due to the sign of "an era that confuses culture with bureaucracy and employs cultural policies to rationalize its own lack of meaning."[17]

CULTURAL DIVERSITY
AND CRITICAL PLURALISM

The problematic of democratic culture is generally summed up as an issue of cultural democratization: that is, as the problem of how to increase the mass population's levels of access to those cultural goods that form part of the artistic patrimony of national culture. Insofar as it is a "model of cultural politics," cultural democratization "has the objective of distributing the capital and the cultural accumulation that exists in society. It is a question of an extensive proposal that seeks to facilitate the majority's access to cultural goods, goods that preferentially include the forms of artistic expression legitimated by tradition. It is a question, as well, of achieving a better geographic and social distribution of the infrastructure through which those goods circulate (cinemas, libraries, bookstores, etc.)."[18]

But the broadest sense of cultural democracy will have failed if the policies seeking a more egalitarian redistribution of social consumption are not concerned at the same time with stimulating mechanisms for creative participation in the process of elaborating and defining the socially active registers of art and culture, which comprise the base of symbolic material from which society conceptualizes itself. Democracy should be not only "cultural plurality" but also "interpretive polysemia,"[19] in terms of its disposition toward opening up current significations to a diversity of points of view, modeling various and variable ways of understanding social reality and its cultural symbolizations. This practice, which consists of multiplying readings and confronting various interpretations, is only possible if zones of critical debate are activated. Zones for reflection and for engaging polemical questions about the organization of cultural discourses and the elaboration of artistic messages according to codes that must be permanently reevaluated from the point of view of what they include or exclude. These necessary zones of debate and reflection have become completely secondary in Chile today, with relation to the other dimensions of art and culture that daily monopolize the resources and attention of the public scene. Images predominate that sublimate art by offering representations of artists and their creations floating on a dematerialized plane, where they fetichistically display an *excess* of sensitivity or imagination destined to retouch —decoratively, "femininely"—social discursivity. The public scene does not conceive of culture as an *intellectual project* or as a *debate of ideas*. It denies culture the capacity for the same density of meanings supposedly contained within political tribunals, which the press and television anoint as the only fora exhibiting real struggles between contending arguments. As Antonio Skármeta states: "In Chile there is no philosophy of cultural action that places creators and their works on a plane as relevant to public life as the one occupied by businessmen, bankers, politicians, and soccer players. The celebration of artists and their work is momentary, meager, and segmented. Intellectuals and artists are cornered in their creation, reduced to solitude, and feel that those in power and the media are indifferent to their presence."[20]

The democratic context has made the dimension of "culture-spectacle" prevail, filled with visibility and mathematical calculation to the point that the complacent symbols of majority culture erase any nuance of critical-reflexive layering and dissipate the ambiguities of everything that does not contribute directly to the performances' show-worthiness. This dimension of the culture-spectacle has privileged a model of pluralism ingratiated to a plurality that unites the greatest diversity of opinions, while taking care to avoid any confrontation of tendencies that might create discord in the equilibrium making differences coexist passively under a neutral regime, all equally aligned under the formula—at once reconciliatory and conciliatory—of the sum total. A formula undoubtedly necessary for exercising tolerance toward a maximum diversity of opinions, but insufficient for that diversity to *articulate* competing readings that design alternative meanings, that empower the confrontational energies of each difference, thus breaking the lax neo-eclecticism of "everything is valid." Only a certain sectarianism of difference ["*partidismo de la diferencia*," Sarlo] could help transform the plural and multiple from an *undifferentiated variety* into a contrasting set of *differentiating variants*, introducing cuts and demarcations of meaning capable of problematizing the most homogenizing tendencies of official pluralism.

In the introduction to her 1990 book on postcoup Chilean literature, which traces the itinerary of the "new scene," Eugenia Brito writes: "I think the period of transition to democracy might generate, in literary criticism, the theoretical framework required for rethinking certain experiences of the country from broader and more integrative perspectives. However, such an integration should safeguard differences: otherwise once again we would fall into a single vision of a process."[21] This call to "safeguard differences" aspires to respect multiplicity and the contradictions of nonuniform artistic sequences and to make room for alternative and divergent strategies of cultural resistance: strategies whose positions and counterpositions have not been sufficiently delineated or confronted. We still lack opportunities for critical debate, for bringing critical gestures "to play alongside, and especially against, each other, to the point of producing an effect that is in none of them and that takes advantage of each of their strengths."[22] Such play appeals to the capacity for articulating "a political gaze" on cultural practices, a gaze capable of focusing on "those discourses, practices, agents, and events that affirm the right to intervene against unification, exhibiting before it the scandal of other perspectives," and that "place forms of dissent in the spotlight."[23] This would provide a means of laterally criticizing the hegemony of the great symbolic and discursive pacts—the market, institutions—that tend to standardize the behavior of cultural reception.

The slogan of recuperation-consolidation of order in this phase of the democratic transition has prioritized the goal of stability, which in turn has tended to postpone differentiating counterpoints. A certain ritualization of consensus has accomplished the elimination of any marks recalling those confrontations of positions that threatened to break with the general will to appease conflicts. Transferred to the field of culture, that slogan of official moderation has favored those practices most in agreement with the new format of national pacification, which calls for *quieting* rather than *disquieting* the order of meaning, and has disfavored those other practices that continue to conceive of language as a zone of disturbances.[24]

There exists a generalized demand for transparent language and direct forms of communication, which obsessively seeks to break with the "obscure formalism" and "contrived aestheticism"[25] imposed by the "extremely intellectualized rhetoric" of the "new scene" in recent years.[26] The weighty burden of critical self-reflexivity entrusted to practices that submitted every conceptual and linguistic mediation of the cultural system to a revision of signs has ended up generating a counterdiscourse of simplification expressed in the call to entertainment, to pleasant banter, and to the gratification of artistic consumption through docile works. Seen from the perspective of literature, today's situation suggests that publishers' recent support of tendencies stimulated by the literary market privileges "conceptions of literature as a product destined for a mass audience that for the most part seeks a conception of the world narrated in representational and realist language, more or less adapted to what is already established,"[27] disregarding those other forms of writing that decenter literary conventions, or that move the signifier through the least frequented shores of the narrative imaginary. Seen from the perspective of the visual arts, the situation also indicates a notorious tendency to sidestep "any critical attempt dedicated to placing the artistic system in crisis," in order to favor instead "reencounters with the public" in terms of "the concomitance between commerce and artistic possession, between production and the market,"[28] leaving the most problematizing works out of the circuit of institutionalvalidation. Experimentation with form, confrontation of styles, and battling codes are seen as operations threatening to fracture and dislocate the "commonplace"–"common sense"[29] of serial thought, produced by cultural institutions and the cultural market's serial products. These operations—which exceed the order of passive significations, creating conflict in its grammar of obedience and discursive conformity—are nevertheless the most capable of experimenting with signs to formulate new points of view about languages and subjectivities that could, in turn, form an active—and questioning—part of a democratic culture of difference(s).

SIX

Conversation: Germán Bravo, Martín Hopenhayn, Nelly Richard, and Adriana Valdés

NR: First I would like to thank each of you for your interest in the book and your willingness to participate in this conversation. We've had the opportunity to share, over the years, several dialogues about culture and the idea here is, simply, to take up again some of those things we've thought about and discussed regarding issues that, in one way or another, appear throughout this book. Adriana is very familiar with the artistic and literary practices whose trajectory the book traces; she has written about several of the works that I analyze and about the scene of which they form a part. Martín, Germán, and I have frequently discussed the problem of the relationships between culture and politics, between aesthetics and social sciences, and we also have questioned more than once the role of the critical intellectual in the context of the democratic transition and posttransition. So, I suggest we revisit these topics, as they emerge through the comments your readings of this book elicited.

AV: I would like to begin the conversation with the subject of citation, as a more or less personal way to situate myself vis-à-vis the book. This always happens to me with Nelly's texts; on the one hand, I'm very interested in being quoted there because she gives the words chosen an existence that those words alone, homeless, perhaps did not have before. On the other hand, though, I always feel a bit torn by the text. A certain small friction always occurs between what is incorporated as a citation and the text itself. For example, this happens when she quotes a portion of my work that functions more as a strategy of defense (rather than offense), and then situates it in the context of a kind of guerrilla group, in the process of constructing the front lines of her text. This gesture at once makes me uncomfortable and interests me, strikes me as very provocative.

MH: I think quotations always decontextualize. Besides, there is an explicit reference to quotation in this very text, where it is presented as one strategy for fragmenting a whole, for introducing and recontextualizing fragments within another whole, and so forth. But Nelly's book has a very particular system of citation. It appears as if the text generates a collective movement through quotation, because for the most part it does not cite materials with which it disagrees, but rather materials that lean in its direction. The prevalent sensation this generates is that the authors quoted and the text all belong to the same tribe.

AV: I like Martín's notion of tribe very much. It also takes me back to a still recent past in which the collective experience of many people, beyond any personal agenda, was the fragmentation of every form of social life and the recomposition of the most primitive units: my people, my tribe. But I remember that in our case it was a strange tribe, whose members didn't recognize one another. Expanding on Martín's idea, it seems to me that this text does in fact express a collective, but it's a collective that establishes its existence within the text more than outside it, and that recognizes itself more a posteriori than it ever did at the time or in reality. At that time, individual intentions simply didn't come together: the movement of ideas perceptible here comes from a very effective way the text has of joining things to make them fit within its own movement. What one individual says in one place appears elsewhere in another's voice, a voice that one would not have imagined. Then a recognition effect is produced: it seems as though a continuity of intentionality must have existed after all. The text enacts the operation of weaving together a collective of individuals; and that operation is very important because, as we know, our scene was one of people with dispersed actions and intentions. Sometimes I ask myself if it's still like this, beyond the glossier surfaces that are so valued today. In any case, it's comforting to feel part of a tribe that once existed—and it would be better yet if it existed still.

NR: I think the citation process has various meanings. On the one hand, I quote many "new scene" texts whose existence did not go beyond a photocopy or a very restricted publication circuit because of their social marginality under authoritarianism. So there's the idea of a kind of rescuing and salvaging that makes me feel like I have to quote these sublocal materials (still foreign to historical registers) whenever I can, because it's the only way of not contributing to the complete disappearance of that critical memory, the most disperse and fragmentary of all. On the other hand, the quotations also obey the desire to carry out a gesture almost exactly the inverse of the compartmentalizing and disconnecting gesture that isolated our practices for so many years, and to create zones of disciplinary intersections, between art or literature and the social sciences, for example, in order to put materials in contact that had not had many opportunities to exchange their signals.

GESTURES OF RESISTANCE VERSUS
DISCOURSES OF ORDER

MH: Now, taking up the matter of content, I would like to pose something that worries me about the relationship between culture and politics, about the tension between acts of resistance and discourses of order, since this is like a matrix that extends throughout the text.

The actors one could identify, and that the text identifies, as actors on the "other shore," that of resistance, of the interstices, of subversion or transgression, are actors who, within the trajectory of the authoritarian order, belonged to the counterhegemonic, to the silenced, the repressed, to that which had no public visibility. With the advent of political democracy, one of the problems I observe, present in the text and which we could discuss further, is the extreme transparency of a democracy in which everything can become visible. There is a market-driven order, an order of consumption, of incorporation of all content into an advertising aesthetic. This creates a kind of obesity of meaning, a hypertransparency that makes it increasingly difficult to reclaim the invisible, the repressed, that which could serve as a point of departure for conceptualizing a discourse of resistance, for producing alternative meanings. An excess of visibility is produced that, moreover, renders everything banal, as the text itself states.

The strategy of irruption or fissuring meets an additional challenge, then: that of being able to "darken" the excess of light into which this combination of political aperture and advertising extroversion has thrown us. Following the light-darkness metaphor, it almost could be said that the tensions are inverted: the subversion of public discourse no longer manifests itself as flashes of light in a world basically dark, but rather as regions of shadow in a reality overexposed to information, the thematization and digestion of signs and symbols. It's not the first time in history that countercultural strategies (or those of cultures of resistance) have had to be rethought because what lies before them has metamorphosed. It is no longer repression that must be defied or revealed. Now they have to confront precisely that which eludes confrontation, namely, the mechanism of recuperation/neutralization of all messages by the status quo: a decentered mechanism, with no fixed countenance, with enclaves spread out everywhere. Within this frame, critical practices have to resituate their forms of interpellation and positioning. To move from victimization to irony, for example . . .

NR: We are indeed submerged in a demand for total visibility that would seem to exclude those critical practices that seek to create opacities or refractions, to show that not all bodies in the system are translucent. But I don't think that this spotlight of hypervisibility encompasses everything equally. Some zones are always less clear than others, slippery zones that escape closed definitions or postulate certain imprecisions or ambivalences of meaning as a way to defy classificatory divisions and overly sharp limits. To invert the direction of the spotlight—almost always placed to represent the eye of the market—and illuminate, if only for a while, the most stubborn practices located outside the spotlight, out of focus, can prove a valuable critical gesture. A gesture that makes evident and virtually opens to debate the ways of seeing that are privileged daily on the system's screens and shopwindows.

It's no longer a matter of rescuing practices from the dark shadows of repression or authoritarian control because, apparently, there is no longer anything completely shadowed in our sparkling democratic landscape—although there are still darker and more enigmatic border zones. Such border zones are never "front page" material because what they suggest goes against the call for "no ambiguity" promoted by the transparency of the system and the market. The challenge always exists, I think, for a critical practice to point out the conflicting points of view that traverse those regions of the system of cultural representation that most believe to be smooth, homogenous, transparent. Critical practice gives those conflicts a symbolic form that serves to take away the innocence of the gaze, even if only partially, because those practices no longer proceed by substituting one (negative) totality of order for another (positive) one, but rather by generating certain interstitial ruptures in hegemonic messages.

GB: I agree with Martín that a dimension of the repressed has now entered a society of spectacle that assimilates everything. But I think there's more to this. It seems to me that part of the strength of what Nelly analyzes in the "poetics of the crisis" stems from an aesthetic of the fragment that, as she says, continues to have critical potential.

The critique of totality and of seamless identities produced by the aesthetic of the fragment reveals a kind of active negativity or representational flaw that, in this image- and communication-driven society, is revealed in a particularly significant way. It makes visible, in the domain of what we call "culture," those fissures and points of disjunction in which society does not completely coincide with itself. In this new setting, the very notions of scene (what is the drama, and what is its style: melodrama, psychodrama?) and of representation (with what language can one name the drama or the nondrama: with the language of philosophy, ecclesiastical catechism, video clips, or comics?), of actor (who acts, and in the name of what principles?), and of author (who writes, and what theory of enunciation serves as the text's point of departure?) all remain suspended. And with the generalized instability of these components of the representational system, "criticism" and "culture" also change places, meanings, and methods. Our reflection today is, in part, an attempt to begin discovering new forms for the practice of cultural criticism, a criticism that, in a certain way, speaks of the originating, insuturable gaps in representations of identity and of the social.

MH: That's true. It's not only a matter of breaking the "complacency of transparency" through opaque zones or with discursive proposals less easily recuperated by the political-advertising *logos* that rules the country. In Nelly's book, it's also about opposing the interstitial to the finished, as Germán says, or the fragment to the system, the inconclusive to the pretension of finished identities. What's happening currently is that, in the tension between politics and culture, it appears that politics imposes on culture a simulated transparency in which everything would seem to lead, as with a funnel, toward its immediate consecration via television, conferences, or state-related mechanisms (despite the fact that there are those who resist this tendency from within the State itself). In this sense, transparency assumes a consecrating slant, once again confusing the political with the cultural: because within the political, to be sure, after so many years of forced silence and invisibility, irruption into the public sphere should become an object of institutionalization. But sometimes it is expected that that same rationale will be applied to the cultural sphere, disregarding the fact that there are very big differences between the two fields. Add to this the moral battle being waged within and outside the Church, which inscribes a contradiction in the midst of this transparency, since the agents of moral conservatism have the intention of overwhelming the public-cultural sphere and imposing a new form of silence on those who oppose them.

NR: A new aspect introduced into the relationship between culture, politics, and society with the democratic reaperture is institutional participation and access to the public sphere by actors who had been marginalized from both. Under authoritarianism, oppositional culture and politics shared equally repressed and compressed zones. Both fought, in an interconnected way, for the expansion of those zones. But the recomposition of the field of these forces in the democratic transition has been asymmetrical. Today, the forced equation between politics and society is total: the political and economic have overwhelmed every representation of the social, with television as their ally, simulating the effect of a perfect redundancy between these three terms. Meanwhile, culture continues to occupy a completely restricted and minority position. Today, economic-political discursivity is the "totality" that art and culture must tear, split, fracture, etc., in order to render audible other voices that might broaden or overflow that frame, a frame of exclusions and compromises made in the name of social modernization.

AV: Now, if we try to speak about transparency at the level of the visual, the theme of the all-encompassing gaze appears. This theme can be addressed from various perspectives. I propose two: one is related to the practices Nelly's book analyzes, which I think always resist that possibility. The other is the panoramic gaze that the social sciences tend to adopt.

To begin, and taking up a phrase used in this conversation, the practices Nelly analyzes share in the "creation of opacities" through their opposition to a supposed transparency. That is, in many of them there is the realization that the gaze does not see it all; or that what it sees is a trompe l'oeil, or that there are things underneath that the gaze doesn't see. I'm thinking, for example, of Dittborn's work with the photographic plot: there we have an effort to work with the gaze of the spectators, who are forced to have the sensation that they don't see what they see, who think they are seeing a smooth surface and in reality are seeing a collection of dots. This is an example on the physical plane, but if we transfer it to another, conceptual plane, it seems that one sees but makes mistakes in seeing, and that the gaze is infinitely problematic, that it can always go beyond itself, give more of itself by pausing before what lies in front of it, educate itself in the etymological sense. The function of these creative practices of opacity is to signal the limitations of sight, make one distrust the immediate gaze, make one doubt the ability to see. It's then that what appears most transparent becomes the most mysterious.

NR: It seems to me that we could insert a distinction between transparency, visibility, and representation. "Transparency" is the illusion that the codes of signification are abstract, neutral, and indeterminate. In speaking of "visibility," we refer to how certain figures acquire a presence, stand out among others, and prevail in a particular field of social vision. And "representation" is the operation of using codes made of signs to construct and produce these effects of presence and signification.

Critical practices move among these three registers. First, they undo the ideological assumption of the effect of transparency, demonstrating the constructed and artificial character of signs through cultural mediations. Second, they open for discussion the rules and limits of the dominant code of visibility: they reveal its arbitrariness, question its hierarchies, etc. And, third, critical practices take apart and rearticulate strategies for the staging of cultural bodies and signs, play with their politics and with their rhetorical tactics and languages. So there's a fairly subtle play, between the lines, that goes beyond the simple verification that everything visible is transparent or that only the visible can be represented.

THE CRITICAL TENSION BETWEEN THE SOCIAL SCIENCES AND CULTURAL PRACTICES

GB: Moving on to another subject, I think one of the great merits of Nelly's work is that it makes visible differences of opinion that for the first time enable debate. The critical tension between the social sciences and other discourses had not previously been shown as conflicting. I think that the reflection Nelly poses and provokes regarding the "new scene" and the social sciences—with its incomplete bridges, its cast nets, deaf points, blind spots, its crying out and listening from afar—could prove particularly fruitful in the new context of the posttransition.

MH: But it's a debate in which it's very difficult to take a position. The discussion needs to be more nuanced because conflicting lines of reasoning also exist within the social sciences. On the one side, we have a whole tradition of critical and self-critical social sciences whose protagonists belonged to the left and who now tend more toward functionalism. They have been accused of a certain pragmatism for having reinserted themselves in the current regime as part of the status quo, albeit while conserving a certain capacity for critique. Some of them are even cited within the text as part (or not part) of the tribe. And on the other side are the social sciences of an entrenched left, a left that refused to cede or shift positions, that represents the political force that least wants to be integrated into the current regime, but with which one cannot identify, either, if one wants to produce a critical discourse or one with emergent meanings. So this supposed tribe would be situated outside both tendencies.

NR: I don't think it's as much a matter of taking a position, as of recognizing and understanding that a certain field of debate has been opened, one that poses an interesting reflection on the subject of the relationships, very often conflictive, between technical rationality and symbolic-expressive flows, or rather between the specialization of disciplinary territories and the dispersed energy of certain extra-systematic readings . . . What I intended in the book was to sharpen certain points, reintensify certain cuts, to try to bring new energy to zones of tension whose critical potential still seems blocked due to a lack of new readings.

I think the text makes it sufficiently clear that, in the case of the tensions we are discussing, it is obviously the more critical tendency in the social sciences that is taken into account in order to consider its representatives as potential interlocutors, and to signal the rather frustrated nature of the dialogue. But it is also true that further nuance is necessary, even within this same tendency. For example, Brunner's quotations come and go throughout the text, in sometimes contradictory directions. Among the social scientists, Brunner's case seems special to me, not only from the perspective of his contributions to intellectual creation, but also because there are certain cracks between the parts and the whole of his texts, which he himself engages in order to subject his own condition as an intellectual to self-critical reflection. These cracks prove quite valuable for analyzing the current situation of intellectuals in Chile, in its more complex and less complacent dimensions.

AV: The intersection between the text and Brunner's quotations made me think about two literary titles: Difficult Loves by Italo Calvino, I believe, and Flaubert's Sentimental Education. In effect, I'm thinking about that dialogue, the attempt to create zones of disciplinary interactions. It's an entire, sometimes disheartening, process. Despite the meager results until now, it seems to me that interest in it remains.

GB: From my point of view, the dialogue with the social sciences proved difficult because what the sociology of culture provided during the dictatorship in Chile was, on the one hand, a kind of description of the transformations the national cultural field underwent in terms of its relationship to the State, the market, and the expansion of the cultural industries—this was especially true of Brunner's work. And, on the other hand, it offered a kind of analysis of Latin American identity—which was the case with Morandé and his school.* But neither advanced a hermeneutic or a critique of works or of aesthetic production. Even the description of the cultural field was paradoxical because it was done in terms of cultural consumption and the market, on the one hand criticizing the censorship and repression of authoritarianism, but at the same time, on the other, repeating the very same categories of the market and cultural industries. This is the paradox that Nelly's text makes visible.

Likewise, Brunner's and Lechner's ambiguities vis-à-vis the "postmodern agenda" also reveal the difficulty for dialogue between the social sciences and the new artistic proposals Nelly analyzes. In my opinion, Brunner and Lechner take on the postmodern agenda, but only from the prism or the question of the political-institutional as the determining or "overdetermining" question of the dictatorship and transition periods. And taking that question as the point of departure, one reaches a point where the postmodern agenda no longer works, or can't be followed, because how can social integration and order be achieved, or how can one make sense of action and social order, from a perspective whose very point of departure is the crisis of all orders of meaning, the crisis of those narratives that grant meaning to actors' identities and actions?

There is, therefore, a fundamental difference between the concept of culture that Nelly is working with and the concepts of culture and politics with which Brunner and Lechner work. And one of the most relevant dimensions of this book is how it elaborates a concept of "critical culture" that is hardly present in either the national or Latin American contexts, that is, as a critique of language, a critique of signs and of representation. There are deep sociological roots for this in the Chilean case. I think that just as Portales can be seen as a kind of paradigm for the political-institutional, Andrés Bello appears as the paradigm of a notion of culture based on the prevention of "orgies of the imagination" (following the formula he used in his polemic against romanticism), a prevention that in the long run operates as a fearful, if not authoritarian, cult to classicism, a dread of ridicule, and an obstacle to originality and creative individuation.[†] The regrettable state of aesthetic critique in Chile's public sphere today expresses, in my opinion, that refusal of the national cultural field to dialogue with new aesthetic currents and to incorporate them as active elements into culture.

AV: I would like to add something to what Germán said about the difficult loves this type of cultural criticism has had with the social science practices that could have been most akin to it in the current or recent Chilean context. I agree that they pursued different objectives. And I would add that they also looked at different things, fundamentally at culture as an industry in the case of some of Brunner's work, or "cultural" forms not at all linked with the kinds of practices this book takes up, but rather with collective forms of coexistence and sensibility within ideological currents, as we heard at one point from Garretón, for example, speaking of Chilean culture. So perhaps they were being asked for something they couldn't and didn't want to deliver.

But I would like to signal a more radical tension. Maybe I'm mistaken, but I think that the practice of the social sciences (for better or worse, they are called sciences) is deeply tied to a way of seeing that has to do with the panoramic, with perspective, with the preference for tracing above all else a line on the horizon that can serve to put all the elements of the landscape in order. I say this without irony. Work in these disciplines takes from them the ruler and compass with which they aspire to construct a delimited space within which to order and classify—tasks necessary for constructing a version, a feeling that one understands something, that is, encompasses it. The ways of ordering that landscape (using which ruler, which compass?) are, in fact, conventional: the conventions of the work are usually explicitly formulated when it is proposed, as well as why precisely those tools are used in that case, and not others that might be found in the bricoleur's toolbox. The elements observed start to be placed in order according to that line traced on the horizon, according to how the territory was delimited, or, to put it more bluntly, how the playing field was drawn. The movement is, then, from the general to the specific, and the specific is dutifully situated in its place. It sounds uncomfortable for the specific, and in effect, it is. Hence the tension. It's painful to find a work seen only partially, forced to fit in a place not precisely its own, stuck at times in a Chinese slipper. It seems to me that the cultural criticism put forth in Nelly's book develops a completely opposite trajectory. It stems from the specific; it takes recourse a posteriori to more general schemes of order (it couldn't do otherwise without refusing to interpret altogether). But it studies the works from the horizons they themselves propose, and its trajectory is therefore more uneven and discontinuous, a gesture in itself more problematizing and less functional or, better yet, professionally dysfunctional. The work is taken up in its moment of symbolic vacillation, when one does not know into what system it should be integrated, in which a picture incompatible with that line on the horizon can be discerned. From the other perspective, structured previously by the gesture of the social sciences I have been trying to describe, the work is taken up in its moment of symbolic appropriation and is assigned to a scheme from which only some of its possibilities for signification are realized. I'd like to pose that tension. I think that both gestures are mutually necessary but that "their desires cross without ever finding each other" (the phrase, taken from another context, is Sonia Montecino's).

SOCIAL INTEGRATION, CULTURAL DEVELOPMENT, AND CRITICAL CULTURE

MH: The situation is that it's very difficult in the social sciences to break through a certain parameter outlined by a very strong symbolic order, according to which politics is responsible for unity and the market is responsible for difference (and here difference is understood, in market fashion, as the differentiation of products, consumer goods, etc). So it's very difficult to break through that kind of symbolic fence and respond to the question we're asking ourselves here: what strategy of difference, within this symbolic order, can illuminate various zones, displace the gaze, change perspectives? How to pose difference within a market that has instituted itself as a mechanism of differentiation, reinforced daily through constant consumption? It's necessary—and worth the redundancy—to distinguish between difference and differentiation. They seem to be neighboring categories but can sometimes be opposites.

While differentiation via the market tends increasingly to restrict the field of singularity to a hypergregarious ritual (for instance, think about shopping centers), difference seeks precisely to rescue singular orders, to intervene with its indissoluble codes in a sort of aseptic fair attended every Sunday by the flocks, a sort of mass after Sunday Mass (where shopwindows provide the altar). In the exhaltation of mercantile visibility, there's nothing more than a complacent sublimation of every plurality. The renovation of products is confused with a wealth of expression, publicity with creativity, differentiated consumption with an autonomous will.

On the one hand, one could object that there's an excessive unification of meaning through political rituality and compulsory consensus. But, on the other, difference is not synonymous with dissent. Because dissent is posed by the Communist Party and by the priest

Pizarro who electorally represents it, even as he embodies at the very same time the most traditional and conventional aspects of the national imaginary.‡ In short, it's difficult, with regard to the market, to confront differentiation because it simulates difference through strategies of hyperidentification; and, with politics, it's also difficult to confront consensus with simple dissent, because it very easily assumes the character of entrenchment, rigidity, and resistance to anything new.

NR: I think what Martín is saying is important, about not confusing "difference," as a value of the critical breaking of uniformity, with "differentiation," as an artificial fabrication of differences through a sort of market cosmetics destined only to stimulate variety in consumption. But, in the case of critical practices, there is also the problem of being able to convert differences into "interferences." It's not only about expressing those differences preconstituted in the social world (differences of gender, race, class, etc.), valuable as those commitments — made in solidarity with the identity politics of the groups representing them — are for articulating connections of spaces and practices. It's also about doing this by producing certain zones of alteration or disorderings of preconstituted forms that represent the world according to official versions, so that what's different, other, emergent, really be available to be read in a tension of signs with what's identical, repeated, the same. I think that critical practice can only pose "difference" (as something to be produced, not expressed), provoking certain conflicts of representation in the codes of cultural signification.

AV: I don't see any special privilege in the gesture of interference or disordering, in and of itself. That makes me think in terms of fixation and confrontations among discontinuous things. I tend to think instead in terms of a trajectory, of continuous movement. "The identical," "the repeated," "the same" do not exist, except when frozen (photographed) in a moment, though in reality that moment is part of a flow. Things surge forth, become established, become formalized; at the same time, they die upon becoming formalized, and the new things that surge forth become modified and more complex—

progressively adjusting, in effect. There's a moment in which what seemed to be shared stops being satisfactory, becomes tired, is perceived as stiff in the joints, is no longer believed; that means it is changing. "The official versions" actually are artificially frozen, caricatures. We all participate in them, and we all separate ourselves from them, and that's part of our being cultural subjects.

I think, on the other hand, that one can speak of various cultural planes and that at this point in the conversation it would be appropriate to distinguish them. One is culture as an accumulation of that which already exists: a set of goods to which large groups can accede, that can be transmitted, becoming reelaborated from generation to generation, but that in the end constitute a stockpile. And the other consists of a cultural margin, which has the dynamism of a small group, is recently elaborated, has not yet entered that collective stockpile, and is a field of experimentation and polemics. Perhaps thinking about culture only in terms of controversy and questioning is excessively partial, apart from being monotonous and tiring. Problematization is absolutely necessary, but it's not everything.

NR: When speaking about the identical and the repeated, I'm not thinking about those terms as something static, invariable, definitive. The identical and the repeated are constructions and productions of effects, with everything that implies about their being socially active and, therefore, mobile. But a social grammar of signs in movement is at the same time destined to produce a certain stereotyping of language, in the sense addressed by Barthes when he pointed out that a stereotype is the freezing of meaning in the mold of a serially produced form, the standardization of the commonplace. The "official versions" are precisely those that don't examine or question that repetitive mechanism of stereotypes, of routine expression worn thin by conformist uses of words or images. It is not difficult to realize that this exists on many levels, including, of course, the level of contestatory discourses, which also possess their own orthodoxies of language.

GB: In relation to what Adriana is pointing out, that it's not about a strategy of cultural destabilization, a sort of cultural terrorism, I also experienced a concern as I read the text. I think that the "sectarianism of difference" Nelly speaks about can suddenly sound like voluntarism if it's not recontextualized. It's necessary to take into account the general mood of Chilean society in order to comprehend this society's resistance to assimilating or elaborating any concept of crisis or critique. The fear of a return to the original trauma is strong, together with the fact that, after a predominance of the death impulse, society tends to invest its libido in order, in the family and institutions, and so forth. Society's libidinal self-satisfaction is such that all negativity is expelled, eliminated as an abnormal reminder of a past that's hoped to be forgotten. Confidence is placed—as in a vote of confidence—in the new moral leadership and in a new institutional system destined to administer development and democracy. In that context, the humor, parody, and euphoria present in many "culture-spectacles" may be more akin to the general mood of the culture than those gestures mobilized by the "poetics of the crisis," marked by an aesthetic of fracturing. There is a transition and a translation under way. Nelly's text itself may be seen as a transitional work, a text that achieves its own transition. The text's gesture is interesting because it implies a retrospective look at the scene of the 1980s, charged with a sort of critical melancholy, but at the same time it is a text that asks itself how to recuperate that critical force in the new context. That's where there is a process of translation and transition under way, given that the actors, themes, and settings of the posttransition are in a state of emerging, as are, along with them, the forms of critical practice.

I don't think that the central problem we face is that of an "officialism" impeding the emergence of new voices. New voices have to emerge from the fissures and contradictions of a type of society and actors that currently are becoming consolidated. Thus there is a problem of temporality and of institutionality for those new voices to emerge and be heard, or for hearing old voices again. Otherwise, the discourse of cultural criticism falls into a void, inasmuch as it doesn't synthesize the themes and moods of society. Democracy, development, and social integration appear as yearnings long worked toward by the national community after decades in which the very existence of that community was dramatically held in suspense. After the violence and horror, a certain complacency, a desire for peace, and a reconciled libido take hold.

NR: I think it's evident, returning to Adriana's and Germán's points, that the entire cultural field can't become transformed into pure instability or pure destabilization, above all in the postdictatorial phase of recuperating normalcy in the social order. There are priorities necessarily related to the task of (re)constructing institutional schemes. But right now, what we call "critical debate" takes place in cultural spaces with tightly circumscribed rules of articulation and functioning, due to the very sectorialization and professionalization of the cultural field. In that sense, it worries me that this discussion about the text hasn't situated it in the more specific context to which it belongs. The defense of certain artistic and literary practices in this text is none other than a critical wager formulated through a reading exercise, one of many, that dialogues and competes in the supply of meanings with the rest of those sharing the same field. It isn't a program of generalized subversion or a model for cultural action for the new times.

Now, it is true that I give the text's tone a certain charge when I speak of the "sectarianism of difference," but I feel that I'm doing this in inverse proportion to the predominant intonation in these years, one of an all-too-complacent pluralism, with a facile rhetoric of variety and diversity, unfurled spectacularly across the entire mercantile facade of the culture-event. I don't think it's up to critical practice to synthesize the entire range of attitudes supposed to be representative of society in general, although this collective disposition obviously influences the conditions for social reception of those practices. It seems to me that the gesture of a critical practice instead leans toward testing the limits of acceptance of the system, its comprehensiveness or its tolerance, by exerting certain pressures of meaning against their internal and external contours in order to modify them. While the integrating tendency of cultural development tends to underscore and reinforce those limits, cultural criticism would tend instead to displace them, submit them to further discussion. Both practices are necessary, but it would seem that there's currently too much enthusiastic agreement about paying attention only to cultural development's normalizing and consolidating functions.

GB: I don't think that one should speak about the dimension of "cultural development" only as a consolidation of the limits of the system. I think that within that notion, as in the notion of social integration, there's a tension between distinct forms of socialization of knowledge systems or of cultural diffusion. There can be forms that are traditional, passive, and authoritarian, with vertical hierarchies, or more active forms that stimulate protagonism and creativity within more horizontal frameworks. Cultural criticism, by contrast, is concerned with inventing knowledge systems, situating itself in the interstitial points where languages are created, including the forms of institutionalization and socialization of those languages. For this reason, the dialectic between "cultural development (or integration)" and "cultural criticism" cannot be determined a priori as an abstract concept, but rather within a concrete social plot. In this sense, I think that the "Chilean case" raises interesting possibilities for a rich interaction between both dimensions, where the intent to foment more protagonistic modes of participation and more critical content in cultural diffusion is evident.

MERCANTILE HYPERVISIBILITY AND CRITICAL STRATEGIES

MH: I insist that the greatest difficulty is that we are paralyzed by double messages and mixed messages, like a schizophrenic. Let's take, for example, the theme of memory with which this book begins. In said theme, there is, on the one hand, a struggle for the appropriation of meaning, for collective interpretation, for making sense of memories that are escaping, and for making visible what had been repressed. But, on the other hand, one could pose the question as well—in a different sense, in the most Nietzschean sense of the phrase "autopoietic forgetting"§—of the possibility of creating through forgetting, through deconditioning and exercising freedom with regard to the past. But one can't favor forgetting, either, even in the spirit of contributing new meanings, because doing so is to side with Parque Arauco[||] and with indulgence in the face of torture and institutionalized crime.

An illustrative case is what happened with Dorfman's play (touched on in Nelly's book).[#] Why did Dorfman's play go unnoticed in Chile? One could respond with what is heard from time to time, namely, that Chileans weren't prepared to see themselves reflected at that moment because they were eluding historical memory. But one could also think about the opposite interpretation: that there have been so many books and testimonios recounting repression that they have wound up neutralizing the impact of themes like the violation of human rights. This is serious, but it's true.

NR: Yes, but I think that in the case of Dorfman's play the answer lies elsewhere, at least for those more specialized audiences familiar with the experimental practices of the last few years. Dorfman's play speaks about memory through a representational apparatus that other Chilean artistic practices already had deconstructed critically. And the greater complexity of signifying operations in that critique makes demands on Dorfman's play that it cannot satisfy, making the play appear naive.

So, returning to the question of visibility and memory: there is an official positioning of the theme of Memory established by the libretto of the democratic transition but, at the same time, no analytical review of those artistic practices that have the most to tell us about the problematics of memory has been taken on within the sphere of cultural reflection.

AV: I'd like to broaden the context of what Nelly's saying. She analyzes the case of Dorfman's play very well, but I'd like to add to her analysis that the interlocutor of that play is not the Chilean left, neither its entrenched sectors nor the others. That play is not situated in relation to local controversies, but rather to the demands of a transnational cultural industry, of a global context. In that setting, local subtleties (and truths) tend to become schematic to the point of disappearing. What's needed there is currency that circulates easily, that is capable of mobilizing the stereotypes commonly held by a North American, mostly academic, left, as well as those present in the theater and now the film industries. One of those stereotypes is an enormous preference for intervening in conflicts that take place at a convenient distance and that can be looked at with a certain moral superiority. That's an almost mechanical gesture activated by Dorfman's play. Another quite stereotypical gesture, and for that reason quite effective, is found in Isabel Allende's work, which offers the North its quota of magic. The two are sure bets in the United States and on the international market, at least in those parts of it most reflecting U.S. influence. To introduce complexities on a local scale — our demand, so absurd, that these works correspond somewhat to the collective experience we've lived through — perhaps would be too much to ask, and furthermore would turn out to be dysfunctional with respect to the market to which they're addressed. There's room for everything in the market, especially for the stereotyped and best-selling image of Latin America, an image preferred, moreover, by the political elite in this country. In that regard, I see fundamental differences between Dorfman's and Allende's success and, for example, that of José Donoso, who was able to access international circuits in a very different manner, and whose work is still key for thinking about Chile.

MH: I'd like to return to the problem of strategies for discourses of interference. This text points out that one of the characteristics of our new context is the dedramatization of the relationships between culture and politics. I think that Nelly's book itself can be understood as a reaction against that dedramatization because it's a text that gives sustained attention to practices of confrontation. Another possible gesture of interference in this situation is to insist on the boredom produced by the smoothing out of daily and public life. To parody how dull life can become when there's no longer anything dramatic going on between culture and politics.

I insist, however, that it's very difficult to carry out a strategy of interference in a country riddled with schizophrenia. On the one hand, there's a moralizing public discourse that prohibits speaking against the Church if one wants to be a candidate for any office, and, on the other, one is permitted privately to choose among hundreds of brothels in Santiago. On the one hand, there's a very market-oriented discourse and, on the other, a traditional-integrationist discourse. There's schizophrenia between the Church's discourse raised in defense of human rights (which I support) and that Church, which at this moment, via Oviedo, is absolutely repressive on moral matters.** Faced with these double standards, double messages, and double lives, interference runs the risk of winding up being incorporated into an already instituted regime of such double standards, messages, and lives. Among these quite habitual practices of hypocrisy, cynicism, and euphemism, thanks to which schizophrenia is alive and well here, how might one maintain an *effective* interference? Maybe the route is to thematize this very schizophrenia, to confront it with a sarcastic attitude that breaks in by *making visible* the invisible threads that support this double standard, message, and way of life.

GB: Regarding the question Martín poses concerning the schizophrenia of our national culture, I think that the function of cultural criticism is to situate and reveal that "double bind," the contradictory double ties of culture, without proposing voluntaristic or utopian solutions to the contradiction. Instead, cultural criticism should be a mode for learning about schizophrenia and moral contradiction as "natural" dimensions of cultural life, a mode of gentle inquiry into the insuturable character of questions of meaning.

Now, I also wonder about ways of introducing into the market of images and communication, or into the cultural industries field, those messages, content, "alternative" or rupturist languages or forms capable of altering or interrupting—from "within" a system that no longer recognizes inside and outside, center or periphery— the dominant landscape, vision, and discourses. I don't know if that terminology is still valid or operationally useful in a society that has made the market and the "cultural industries" part of its systemic mechanism of integration.

It's true that we're facing the great machinery of "seduction capitalism," as it's been called, but I don't think that cultural criticism should be content with a strategy of "resistance" or of simple "interruption" of what the market sets in motion. There are modes of intervention in the larger space of communication that permit broader dialogues and greater intertextuality among the different languages in use. To some extent, cultural criticism should enter into the game of seduction, the language of desire, that the market actualizes. I think that above all, on the left, there's a rediscovery of the "revolutionary" dimension of the market and of liberalism—because of its capacity to radicalize the interchange of messages, products, and even identities, a capacity to unleash the playful dimension, a dimension of adventure, of creation and invention of subjects. In my view, this requires rethinking the analytical strategies and practices of the 1960s paradigm of "cultural criticism." Sometimes a rather modest, if not idealist, conception of cultural criticism can overlook this object-based dimension—of the object of desire and desire for the object—driven by the market. Cultural criticism should be a sort of analytics of phantasms and fantasy, a critique of the cultural imaginary.

NR: In effect, the categories of center and margins have been redefined in multiple senses that oblige us to rediagram the relationships between culture and institutions in a much more diagonal form than before. There is no longer any exteriority to the system, which doesn't mean that there aren't always zones that are less valued and favored than others in relation to symbolic hierarchies, or that those disaggregated zones don't occupy much more marginal positions on the map of cultural exchange. In any event, I don't believe, either, that it's about exercising criticism from the margin as pure externality, but rather about progressively acquiring sufficient tactical mobility to occupy intermediate positions from which to push boundaries and force limits but also combine forces and forge alliances.

Now, I think that Martín's and Germán's points have touched on the key problem: what are the conditions for an effective practice of critical intervention within a system of institutional pluralism and market liberalism, which tends to absorb all signs of difference within a kind of mechanism reconfirming its own logic of indifferentiation? Some think, much like Baudrillard, that any attempt to oppose the system is destined to fail because the system's extreme ability consists precisely of its being able to assimilate and recycle everything (transgressions, subversions, etc.) as inoffensive variants of its own structural game. And that all we can do is be ironic with the code by using the code, leaving afloat a sort of double meaning as the sole mark of parody. But it's very difficult for that gesture not to exhaust itself in a kind of fetishistic imitation, with a more reverent than irreverent wit. It seems to me, on the other hand, that we idealize the system all over again if we think that its logic of recuperation-neutralization is so absolute or that its mechanisms are so hermetically sealed. The range of agents, discourses, and practices that comprise the system of cultural organization always presents more flexible articulations, more worn out pieces or loose gears, that open up possibilities for creating change. The armatures of systems are never so perfect or resistant; not all their parts are coordinated so effectively. Each one of us has been able to confirm many times that, in different institutions, there are those more fragile, precarious, or vulnerable zones, which are the zones to take advantage of for introducing unforeseen, more adventurous or exploratory, gestures.

Although it may be very difficult, it seems to me worthwhile to keep battling for spaces for cultural criticism, above all at a time in which the languages of the economy and of politics saturate the entire context with their market rationales, and that most discussions about culture can be summarized in the bureaucratic-administrative terms of a simple evaluation of cultural policies. Cultural criticism reintroduces a reflexive density into the relationships between culture and society.

MH: I think our situation of double or mixed messages, to which I was referring before, can become paralyzing, placing the critical spirit halfway between a debt to history and an opening to invention. I think that this double message, which I haven't seen referenced in Chilean intellectual discussion, carries a lot of weight in the cultural imaginary of those who align themselves with a nonhegemonic discourse. We are, in a certain sense, oscillating between the symbolic field of human rights and postmodernism's reelaboration of the emancipatory impulse. It's hard for us to produce a synthesis here, and this difficulty speaks very clearly about the cultural substrates that currently move the country. Modernizing triumphalism can be a form of "forward flight" with regard to this tension.

I'd like to take up something that seems attractive to me as a concept, which is what Marcuse called "repressive desublimation" in his critique of consumer society. It's the idea that through a discourse that's based on liberty and tolerance, and counter to censorship, there would always resurface a certain complacency with the status quo and the "establishment." Marcuse saw the system's fierce ability to ensure that the actualization of desires, impulses, and repressed truths would be stamped with the neutralizing imprint of a preformatted reality. I think this applies very much to what's happening in Chile in terms of culture, life, and imaginaries. On the side of politics, everything's open to conversation; and, on the side of culture, we are all modern.

I think that Nelly's text looks for how and where to create spaces in which the aperture of new meanings need not assume the form of an institutionalization of repressed desires. Her text suggests that we are in a regime of such repressive desublimation that it's very difficult to find points of splintering or to activate zones of interference. In this sense, Nelly's book, more than accounting for critical culture, invokes the need to rethink critical culture in an order where new forms of repressive desublimation tend to crop up, and where such desublimation occurs in a climate of hypertransparency, of a new economic rationalization of subjects, and of administrative professionalism in the field of power. The book remains situated, in this way, halfway between a rendering of what culture is as critique and as a zone of interference of discourses, and a summons to rethink this place of interferences in a "successfully" postdictatorial and commercialized order. It doesn't provide answers but questions.

GB: I'm intuiting that what we call the posttransition opens a particularly fertile space for the exercise and development of a practice like the critique of culture. Cultural criticism speaks through the fissures of the myths of a transparent or reconciled society.

With regard to what Nelly said earlier, I think that while her text is inscribed within a textual practice and a critical tradition, the text overflows its field and metaphorizes a relationship between culture and politics that takes on enormous importance today. In a society emphasizing communication, images, and spectacles, the aesthetic field becomes a trench where social conflict and the "struggle for hegemony" are revealed with particular intensity. I always remember Trotsky's phrase from *Problems of Everyday Life*, in which he pointed out that social conflict in developed societies would be concentrated in various schools of aesthetics, forms of educating children, and the colors of peoples' houses. I think that in our contemporary context, without denying hunger and war, the drama tends to be read more and more as an "epistemological drama" (relative to the self-awareness of the species), as an "ethical drama" (relative to the possible norms for coexistence), and as an "aesthetic drama" (the debate concerning expressive forms or dramatic styles).

CONVERSATION PARTICIPANTS

GERMÁN BRAVO received his undergraduate degree in sociology from the Universidad Católica de Chile. He pursued doctoral studies at the École Pratique des Hautes Études en Sciences Sociales and at the Université de Paris III, la Sorbonne Nouvelle. He also obtained a postgraduate diploma in social sciences from FLACSO (Latin American Faculty of Social Sciences). Between 1986 and 1989, he participated in the Jacques Derrida Seminar, École Normale Supérieure in Paris. Currently he teaches sociology at the Universidad ARCIS. His research includes numerous studies in the fields of human rights, social sciences, Latin American thought, and theories of modernization.

MARTÍN HOPENHAYN studied philosophy at the Universidad de Chile, the Universidad de Buenos Aires, and the Université de Paris. He serves as a professor of philosophy at the Universidad de Chile, Universidad Diego Portales, and Universidad ARCIS, as a researcher at CEPAUR (Center for Development Alternatives), and as a consultant for several social science research organizations in Santiago. He currently is a member of the Social Development Division at CEPAL (Economic Commission for Latin America and the Caribbean). He has offered seminars and talks in Latin America and Spain and has numerous publications on the culture of modernity and postmodernity in Latin America.

ADRIANA VALDÉS is the author of essays on visual arts and literature. She began her career as professor of literature at the Universidad Católica de Chile (1965–75). Today she works for an international organization at its headquarters in Santiago. She collaborates with the *Revista de crítica cultural* (Santiago), *Mapocho* (Santiago), *Art nexus* (Bogotá), and other publications. In addition to her texts on art, she has published several essays about women and culture and about women's writing. She is a member of the Chilean Academy of Language.

Notes

Translators' Preface

1 For commentary on Richard's work within the context of Southern Cone culture after 1990, see Francine Masiello, *The Art of Transition: Latin American Culture and Neoliberal Crisis* (Durham, N.C.: Duke University Press, 2001).

2 Nelly Richard, *Residuos y metáforas: Ensayos de crítica cultural sobre el Chile de la transición* [Residues and Metaphors: Essays of Cultural Criticism on Chile during the Transition] (Santiago: Editorial Cuarto Propio, 1998), 13–14. All translations from this text are our own. A translation of this work is forthcoming from the University of Minnesota Press.

3 Ibid., 23.

4 Ibid.

5 Ana del Sarto, "Cultural Critique in Latin America or Latin-American Cultural Studies?" *Journal of Latin American Cultural Studies* 9, 3 (2000): 236.

6 For in-depth studies of Richard's work and its role in the development of Latin American cultural studies, consult the first five articles in the *Journal of Latin American Cultural Studies* 9, 3 (December 2000).

7 Other works by Richard in English translation include *Margins and Institutions: Art in Chile since 1973*, special issue of *Art & Text* 21 (1986); "Reply to Vidal (from Chile)," in *The Postmodernism Debate in Latin America*, ed. John Beverley and José Oviedo (Durham, N.C.: Duke University Press, 1993): 228–31; and "Chile, Women, and Dissidence" (137–44), "Women's Art Practices and the Critique of Signs" (145–51), and "Postmodern Decentrednesses and Cultural Periphery: The Disalignments and Realignments of Cultural Power" (260–69), in *Beyond the Fantastic: Contemporary Art Criticism in Latin America*, ed. Gerardo Mosquera (Cambridge: MIT Press, 1996).

8   Michel De Certeau, "Preface to the English Translation," in *The Practice of Everyday Life*, trans. Steven Rendall (Berkeley: University of California Press, 1984), ix.

ONE   Ruptures, Memory, and Discontinuities

  ★   *Translators' note*: This book was originally published in 1994; hence, Richard refers here to the two decades following the 1973 coup. We have conserved all temporal references to the Spanish-language original throughout this translation but have added brackets or notes to clarify Richard's time-frame for English-speaking audiences.

  1   For a fine analysis of the trope of mourning in postdictatorial memory, see Moreiras, "Postdictadura y reforma del pensamiento."

  †   *Translators' note*: The idea of an "alphabet of survival" begins a metaphor that structures this essay, a metaphor based on building blocks of language including the alphabet, grammar, syntagms, and so on, as reconfigured by the exigencies of postcoup Chile's sociopolitical context. The phrase here may be understood as meaning "linguistic elements composing a new language based on, and necessitated by, survival."

  2   Morales, "Walter Benjamin y la crítica literaria chilena," 217–18.

  3   Benjamin, cited by Morales, "Walter Benjamin y la crítica literaria chilena," 221; translation: Walter Benjamin, "Short Shadows (II)," 699.

  4   Deleuze and Guattari, *Rhizoma*, 60.

  5   Casullo, "Walter Benjamin y la modernidad," 35–36.

  6   Benjamin, "The Work of Art in the Age of Mechanical Reproduction," 218.

  7   Valdés, "Señales de vida en un campo minado."

  8   Ibid.

  ‡   *Translators' note*: Rather than speaking more generically about binary oppositions, Richard uses this language of "YES" versus "NO" to recall explicitly the terms of the 1988 Chilean plebiscite that officially ended the Pinochet dictatorship. She critiques the ways in which this logic has constrained political and cultural discourse during the subsequent democratic transition.

  9   Hopenhayn, "¿Qué tienen contra los sociólogos?" 95.

  10   Eltit, *El padre mío*, 17.

  11   Brito, *Campos minados*, 7.

  12   Ibid., 20.

  13   Oyarzún, "Parpadeo y piedad," 32.

14   These quotes are part of a text by Adriana Valdés about the visual artist Gonzalo Díaz; see "Gonzalo Díaz: Pintura por entrega"/ "Gonzalo Díaz:
Painting on Commission," 16.

15   Ibid.

16   Benjamin, "The Work of Art in the Age of Mechanical Reproduction," 225–26.

17   See Ronald Kay's masterful reflection on the photographic apparatus in *Del espacio del acá.*

18   Benjamin, "Little History of Photography," 527.

19   See Dittborn, *Mapa.*

20   Pastor Mellado, *El fantasma de la sequía,* n.p.

21   Vidal, *Dictadura militar,* 106.

22   Cánovas, Lihn, Zurita, ICTUS, Radrigán, 15.

23   Ibid.

24   Cánovas, "Llamado a la tradición," 20.

25   Ibid.

26   These included Dittborn, *De la chilena pintura historia;* Altamirano, *Revisión crítica de la historia del arte chileno;* and Díaz, *Historia sentimental de la pintura
chilena.*

27   Brito, *Campos minados,* 226.

28   Eltit, *E. Luminata,* 18.

29   Zima, "L'ambivalence dialectique," 134.

30   Yúdice, "Testimonio y concientización," 214.

31   Ibid.

32   Sonia Montecino, "Testimonio y mujer," 122.

33   Eltit, *El padre mío,* 13.

34   Donoso and Errázuriz, *La manzana de Adán / Adam's Apple.*

35   Eltit, *El padre mío,* 12.

36   Muñoz, "El gesto del otro," 25.

37   Piña, foreword to Donoso and Errázuriz, *La manzana de Adán / Adam's
Apple,* 5.

38   Yúdice, "Testimonio y concientización," 214.

§   *Translators' note:* Richard's reference to "nonpacted alternatives" ["*al-
ternativas no concertadas*"] invokes opposition to the official "pacts" of the
Concertación, the coalition of center and left parties that has governed Chile
since 1990. Here, she implicitly impugns its arranged political compromises
and their resultant limitations.

39   Díaz, *Sueños privados, ritos públicos,* n.p.

40   Ibid.

41   Beatriz Sarlo, "La historia contra el olvido," 11–13.

42   Ariel Dorfman's *Death and the Maiden* had its first important staging in London, at the Institute of Contemporary Arts (ICA) in November 1990.

43   Alfredo Castro's *Teatro de la memoria* [Theater of Memory] is composed of a trilogy of plays: *La manzana de Adán/Adam's Apple* (1990), *Historia de la sangre* [History of Blood] (1992), and *Los días tuertos* [One-Eyed Days] (1993).

44   See Boyle, "The Mirror to Nature?"

45   Adorno, *Minima Moralia*, 151.

TWO   A Border Citation

1   Oyarzún, "Arte en Chile de treinta años."

2   Ibid.

3   The *escena de avanzada* [literally, "the advanced scene"; figuratively, the scene at the "front lines" or forefront of art, art's cutting edge] or *nueva escena* [new scene] designates a group of practices that was characterized— within the antidictatorial field—by its neo–avant-garde experimentation. These practices were generated, after 1977, both in art (Eugenio Dittborn, Carlos Leppe, Juan Dávila, Carlos Altamirano, the group CADA, Lotty Rosenfeld, Catalina Parra, Alfredo Jaar, etc.) and in literature (Raúl Zurita, Diamela Eltit, Diego Maquieira, Juan Luis Martínez, Gonzalo Muñoz, Soledad Fariña, etc.), setting forth a critical reconceptualization of the languages, techniques, and genres of art and literature inherited from artistic and literary traditions. This set of practices has been analyzed primarily in Richard, *Margins and Institutions*, and Brito, *Campos minados*.

4   Oyarzún, "Arte en Chile de treinta años."

5   Bürger, "Aporias of Modern Aesthetics," 55.

6   Diamela Eltit, "Sobre las acciones de arte."

7   CADA, "Una ponencia del CADA."

8   Ibid.

9   Gianni Vattimo, *El fin de la modernidad*, 52.

10   Norbert Lechner, "Desmontaje y recomposición," 28.

11   Peter Bürger, "El significado de la vanguardia," 170.

12   CADA, "Una ponencia del CADA."

13   Eugenio Tironi, *La Torre de Babel*, 61.

14   Zurita, *Escrituras en el cielo*.

15   Ibid.

16   CADA, "Una ponencia del CADA."

17   Ibid.

18 Muñoz, "Lo que no nos mata."

19 Ibid.

20 Pérez, "Variaciones sobre un cadáver exquisito."

21 Muñoz, "Lo que no nos mata."

22 Huyssen, "Mapping the Postmodern," 21.

23 Bürger, "Aporias of Modern Aesthetics," 56.

24 Subercaseaux, "Nueva sensibilidad y horizonte 'post' en Chile," 140.

25 Oyarzún, "Arte en Chile de treinta años."

26 Ibid.

*   Translators' note: Richard refers here to the context of the democratic transition and its discourse emphasizing "consensus."

†   Translators' note: In Spanish, pena means "grief," in the sense of "sorrow" or emotional "pain," but it may also indicate a sense of "shame" or "punishment," as in pena de muerte (the death penalty). Although we have chosen the first, this range of meanings—all relevant in a postdictatorial context—should be understood throughout this section.

27 Bravo, "Las nuevas escrituras," 353.

28 Zurita, "Raúl Zurita y su locura de escribir en el desierto."

29 Bravo, "Las nuevas escrituras," 355.

30 Zurita, "Raúl Zurita y su locura de escribir en el desierto."

31 Zurita, "Nace 'la vida nueva.' "

32 Ibid.

33 Zurita, "Raúl Zurita y su locura de escribir en el desierto."

THREE Destruction, Reconstruction, and Deconstruction

1 Brunner, Barrios, and Catalán, Chile, 178.

2 Brunner, Un espejo trizado, 89.

*   Translators' note: The years 1983–84 marked the explosion of national protests against the Pinochet regime. Traditional social actors (e.g., political parties, labor) reemerged at that time, while new social movements (e.g., women's movements) also became widely visible.

3 Garretón, Reconstruir la política, 284.

4 Garretón, El proceso chileno, 188.

†   Translators' note: The acronym MIR stands for Movimiento de Izquierda Revolucionario [Movement of the Revolutionary Left]; it was founded in 1965, inspired by Guevarist views. MAPU stands for Movimiento de Acción Popular Unitaria [Movement for Unified Popular Action]; the acronym is the Mapuche word for "earth." MAPU began in 1969 as a left-

leaning offshoot of the Christian Democratic Party and gave rise in turn to MAPU-OC (Obrero Campesino [Worker Peasant]), focused, as its name suggests, on working- and peasant-class issues.

5 Brunner, *Un espejo trizado*, 395.

6 Ibid., 331.

7 Subercaseaux, *Sobre cultura popular*, 7.

8 Muñoz, "El gesto del otro," 22.

9 Ibid.

10 Oyarzún, "Arte en Chile de treinta años."

11 Ibid.

‡ *Translators' note*: Hopenhayn speaks of "trenches" and "lightning-fast actions" to invoke forms of street action and protest that took place during the dictatorship. These protests, or *manifestaciones relámpago*, typically lasted only a few minutes, with the crowd dissipating as soon as police appeared in the area (usually the center of Santiago).

12 Hopenhayn, "¿Qué tienen contra los sociólogos?" 97.

13 Galaz, *En Tierra*.

14 Ibid.

15 Brugnoli, *Cadáver exquisito*.

16 Brito, *Campos minados*, 191.

17 Oyarzún, "Parpadeo y piedad," 31.

18 Altamirano, *Pintor de domingo*.

19 Bianchi, *Poesía chilena*, 166.

20 Ibid.

21 Brunner, Barrios, and Catalán, *Chile*, 154.

22 Brunner, "Campo artístico," 64–65.

23 Brunner, Barrios, and Catalán, *Chile*, 155.

24 Muñoz, "El gesto del otro," 26.

25 Oyarzún, "Parpadeo y piedad," 31.

26 Muñoz, "Una sola línea para siempre," 57.

27 Lechner, "Desmontaje y recomposición," 26.

28 See Berenguer et al., *Escribir en los bordes*.

29 Brunner, Barrios, and Catalán, *Chile*, 155.

FOUR The Social Sciences

1 Bourdieu, *Sociology in Question*, 139.

2 Cánovas, "Hacia una histórica relación sentimental," 165.

3 Ibid.

4 Oyarzún, "Arte en Chile de treinta años."

5   Cánovas, "Hacia una histórica relación sentimental," 165.

6   Forster, "El encogimiento de las palabras," 34.

7   Brunner, "6 preguntas a José Joaquín Brunner," 23.

8   Ibid., 22.

9   Ibid., 23.

10 Ibid.

11 Hopenhayn, El humanismo crítico, 1.

12 In the case of José Joaquín Brunner, this is corroborated by his initiative in publishing Arte en Chile desde 1973: Escena de avanzada y sociedad, a FLACSO document about the problematic of the "escena de avanzada," bringing together materials from a seminar comprised of artists, theorists, and social scientists; by his interest in the work of Raúl Zurita, who wrote the prologue to [Brunner's] La cultura autoritaria en Chile; and by his collaboration in the publication of Desacato, about the visual artist Lotty Rosenfeld's work.

13 CENECA [Centro de Indagación y Expresión Cultural y Artística / Center for Research on Cultural and Artistic Expression] brought together a group of researchers who, starting in 1977, produced numerous works of cultural sociology, especially in the fields of popular artistic expression, theater, and social communication. However, it is important to highlight a few publications that allowed more specific reflection about the "escena de avanzada" or "new scene" like Aguiló's Propuestas neovanguardistas en la plástica chilena, Cociña's Tendencias literarias emergentes, Zurita's Literatura, lenguaje y sociedad (1973–1983), and Cánovas's Texto y censura: Lihn.

14 Brunner, Barrios, and Catalán, Chile, 155–56.

15 Brunner, "Campo artístico," 65.

16 Ibid., 66.

17 Muñoz, "Manifiesto por el claroscuro," 55.

18 Ibid.

19 Lechner, "Desmontaje y recomposición," 29.

20 Brunner, "Campo artístico," 67.

21 Ibid.

22 Brito, Campos minados, 12–13.

23 Muñoz, "El gesto del otro," 23.

24 Oyarzún, "Crítica: historia," 47.

25 Ibid.

26 Ibid., 48.

27 García Canclini, "Los estudios culturales de los 80 a los 90," 41–48.

28 Brunner, "6 preguntas a José Joaquín Brunner," 24.

29 Hopenhayn, El humanismo crítico, 29.

30 Brunner, Barrios, and Catalán, Chile, 154.

31 Cánovas, "Del debate feminista."

32 Ibid.

33 García Canclini, "Los estudios culturales de los 80 a los 90," 47.

34 Ibid.

35 Ibid.

36 Hopenhayn, "¿Qué tienen contra los sociólogos?" 94.

FIVE Staging Democracy and the Politics of Difference

*   Translators' note: Underscoring this emphasis on compromise, the center-left coalition governing in Chile since 1990 took as its name la Concertación.

1 Garretón, Sosnowski, and Subercaseaux, Cultura, autoritarismo y redemocratización en Chile, 8–9.

2 Rama, "Indagación de la ideología en la poesía," 242.

3 Ibid.

4 Escobar, "Cultura y transición democrática en Paraguay," 33–34.

5 Ibid.

6 García Canclini, Hybrid Cultures, 262.

7 Valdés, "Gestos de fijación, gestos de desplazamiento," 137.

8 Ibid.

9 Brunner, "6 preguntas a José Joaquín Brunner," 21.

10 Sarlo, "Intellectuales," 57.

11 Ibid.

12 Ibid., 58.

13 Garretón, "Los intelectuales han muerto."

14 Altamirano, "El intelectual en la represión y en la democracia," 4.

15 Ibid.

16 Brunner, "Preguntas del futuro," 71.

17 Ibid, 75.

18 Subercaseaux, "Política y cultura," 144.

19 García Canclini, Hybrid Cultures.

20 Skármeta, "Todas las libertades, la libertad," 96.

21 Brito, Campos minados, 12.

22 Valdés, "Gestos de fijación, gestos de desplazamiento," 146.

23 Sarlo, "Intellectuales."

24 This is demonstrated by the inclusion of the topic of the "avanzada" scene on a panel addressing "the incorporation of the margins" (together with women, exile, and indigenous groups) at the seminar "Cultura, auto-

ritarismo y redemocratización" [Culture, Authoritarianism, and Redemoc-
ratization] at the University of Maryland, December 1991.
25 Cárcamo, "La tentación del significante."
26 Cárcamo, "La escena emplazada."
27 Olea, "Brevísima relación de la literatura actual," 142.
28 Ivelic, "La transgresión de los límites," 131.
29 Eltit, "Concerning Literary Practice," 138.

SIX *Conversation*

   ★ *Translators' note:* Pedro Morandé, a conservative Chilean sociologist,
has served as provost and dean of the School for Social Sciences at the Universidad Católica de Chile. His publications include *Iglesia y cultura en América
Latina* (1989; Culture and the Church in Latin America) and *Persona, matrimo-
nio y familia* (1994; Individuals, Matrimony, and the Family).
   † *Translators' note:* Diego Portales (1793–1837) served at different times
as Chile's secretary of state, minister of war, and minister of the interior
and as governor of Valparaiso. He is viewed as a key political "strong man,"
whose philosophy greatly influenced the Chilean constitution of 1833.
Andrés Bello (1781–1865) was the founder of the Universidad de Chile and
the author of Chile's Código Civil [civic code]. An advocate of pan-American-
ism, one of his most important legacies stems from his philosophy of language—in which order would triumph over chaos and difference through
the linguistic unification of Latin America.
   ‡ *Translators' note:* In 1993 the conservative priest Eugenio Pizarro was
chosen to represent one segment of the Communist Party as a candidate for
the Chilean presidency. His bid for that office was unsuccessful.
   § *Translators' note:* The term "autopoietic," from the Greek *poiesis*, refers to the activity of making or producing, as in shaping something out of
malleable material. In the Nietzschean sense, in which people adhere not to
moral values but to aesthetic ones, humans make themselves into objects of
aesthetic value, and in this sense they are autopoietic or autogeneric. Moreover, for Nietzsche, the creative act is an exercise of freedom (though few
ever reach self-actualization). Hopenhayn builds on Nietzsche to suggest
that the creative activity of autogeneric self-construction, as it progresses
into the future, involves forgetting, which is as constitutive of "selfhood" as
what is created out of "present" materials.
   || *Translators' note:* Parque Arauco is a large shopping mall in Santiago,
named, ironically, for the indigenous Mapuches.

\#   *Translators' note*: Ariel Dorfman's *Death and the Maiden* had its Chilean debut at the Teatro de la Esquina in Santiago on March 10, 1991, in the month after the Rettig Commission issued its report on human rights abuses under Pinochet. Directed by Ana Reeves, the play featured María Elena Duvachelle, Hugo Medina, and Tito Bustamante in its three roles. Richard discusses the play in chapter 1.

★★   *Translators' note*: Carlos Oviedo Cavada was named archbishop of Santiago by Pope John Paul II in 1990, and he served in that capacity until a few months before his death in 1998. He was an outspoken conservative critic of Chile's "moral crisis" and caused a public furor in 1994 when he declared that truly Catholic legislators could not vote to legalize divorce.

Bibliography

Adorno, Theodor. *Minima Moralia*. Trans. E. F. N. Jephcott. London: Verso, 1987.

Aguiló, Osvaldo. *Propuestas neovanguardistas en la plástica chilena: Antecedentes y contexto* [Neo-Avant-Garde Proposals in Chilean Art: History and Context]. Santiago: CENECA Document 27, 1983.

Altamirano, Carlos. "El intelectual en la represión y en la democracia" [Intellectuals During the Repression and During Democracy]. *Punto de vista* 28 (1986): 1–4.

———. *Revisión crítica de la historia del arte chileno* [Critical Revision of the History of Chilean Art]. Santiago: Galería CAL, 1979.

———. *Pintor de Domingo* [Sunday Painter]. Santiago: Francisco Zegers Editor, 1991.

Benjamin, Walter. "The Work of Art in the Age of Mechanical Reproduction." In *Illuminations*, ed. Hannah Arendt, trans. Harry Zohn, 217–51. New York: Schocken Books, 1969.

———. "Little History of Photography." In *Selected Writings*, vol. 2, 1927–1934, ed. Michael W. Jennings, Howard Eiland, and Gary Smith; trans. Rodney Livingstone et al., 507–30. Cambridge, Mass.: Belknap Press, 1996.

———. "Short Shadows (II)." In *Selected Writings*, vol. 2, 1927–1934, ed. Michael W. Jennings, Howard Eiland, and Gary Smith; trans. Rodney Livingstone et al., 699–702. Cambridge, Mass.: Belknap Press, 1996.

Berenguer, Carmen, et al., eds. *Escribir en los bordes: Congreso Internacional de Literatura Femenina Latinoamericana* [Writing in the Margins: International Conference on Latin American Women's Literature]. Santiago: Editorial Cuarto Propio, 1990.

Bianchi, Soledad. *Poesía chilena* [Chilean Poetry]. Santiago: Editorial Documentas/CESOC, 1990.

Bourdieu, Pierre. *Sociology in Question*. Trans. Richard Nice. London: Sage Publications, 1993.

Boyle, Catherine. "The Mirror to Nature? Latin American Theatre in London." *Travesía* 1 (1992): 105–17.

Bravo, Germán. "Las nuevas escrituras" [New Writings]. *Utopía(s)*. Santiago: División de Cultura del Ministerio de Educación, 1993: 353.

Brito, Eugenia. *Campos minados* [Mined Fields]. Santiago: Editorial Cuarto Propio, 1990.

Brito, Eugenia, et al., *Desacato: Sobre la obra de Lotty Rosenfeld* [Disrespect: On the Work of Lotty Rosenfeld]. Santiago: Francisco Zegers, 1986.

Brugnoli, Francisco. *Cadáver exquisito* [Exquisite Corpse]. Santiago: Catálago Ojo de Buey, 1990.

Brunner, José Joaquín. *La cultura autoritaria en Chile* [Authoritarian Culture in Chile]. Santiago: FLACSO, 1981.

———. "Campo artístico, escena de avanzada y autoritarismo en Chile" [The Artistic Field, the *Avanzada* Scene, and Authoritarianism in Chile]. In *Arte en Chile desde 1973: Escena de avanzada y sociedad* [Art in Chile since 1973: The *Avanzada* Scene and Society], 57–67. Santiago: FLACSO Document 46, 1987.

———. *Un espejo trizado* [A Shattered Mirror]. Santiago: FLACSO, 1988.

———. "6 preguntas a José Joaquín Brunner" [Six Questions for José Joaquín Brunner]. *Revista de crítica cultural* 1 (1990): 20–25.

———. "Preguntas del futuro" [Questions of the Future]. In *1990–1994: La cultura chilena en transición* [1990–1994: Chilean Culture in Transition], ed. Ana María Foxley and Eugenio Tironi, 71–75. Santiago: Secretaría de Comunicación y Cultura, 1994.

Brunner, José Joaquín, Alicia Barrios, and Carlos Catalán. *Chile: Transformaciones culturales y modernidad* [Chile: Cultural Transformation and Modernity]. Santiago: FLACSO, 1989.

Bürger, Peter. "El significado de la vanguardia" [The Meaning of the Avant-Garde]. In *El debate modernidad/posmodernidad* [The Modernity/Postmodernity Debate], ed. Nicolás Casullo, 161–71. Buenos Aires: Punto Sur, 1989.

———. "Aporias of Modern Aesthetics." *New Left Review* 184 (November–December 1990): 47–56.

CADA (Colectivo de Acciones de Arte [Art Actions Collective]). "Una ponencia del CADA" [A Presentation by CADA]. *Ruptura*. Santiago: Ediciones CADA, 1982.

Cánovas, Rodrigo. Lihn, Zurita, ICTUS, Radrigán: *Literatura chilena y experien-*

cia autoritaria [Lihn, Zurita, ICTUS, Radrigán: Chilean Literature and the Authoritarian Experience]. Santiago: FLACSO, 1986.

———. *Texto y censura: Lihn* [Text and Censorship: Lihn]. Santiago: CENECA Document 77, 1986.

———. "Llamado a la tradición, mirada hacia el futuro o parodia del presente" [Appeal to Tradition, Gaze toward the Future, or Parody of the Present]. In *Arte en Chile desde 1973: Escena de avanzada y sociedad* [Art in Chile since 1973: The *Avanzada* Scene and Society], 17–23. Santiago: FLACSO Document 46, 1987.

———. "Hacia una histórica relación sentimental de la crítica literaria en estos reinos" [Toward a Sentimental History of Literary Criticism in These Kingdoms]. *Cuadernos hispanoamericanos* nos. 482–483 (August–September 1990): 161–76.

———. "Del debate feminista" [On the Feminist Debate]. *Literatura y libros* supplement to *La Epoca* (Santiago), March 1993.

Cárcamo, Luis Ernesto. "La escena emplazada" [The Situated Scene]. *Literatura y libros* supplement to *La Epoca* (Santiago), 29 August 1993.

———. "La tentación del significante" [The Temptation of the Signifier]. *Literatura y libros* supplement to *La Epoca* (Santiago), 5 September 1993.

Casullo, Nicolás. "Walter Benjamin y la modernidad" [Walter Benjamin and Modernity]. *Revista de crítica cultural* 4 (November 1991): 35–40.

Cociña, Carlos. *Tendencias literarias emergentes* [Emergent Literary Tendencies]. Santiago: CENECA Document 31, 1983.

Deleuze, Gilles, and Félix Guattari. *Rhizoma* [Rhizome]. Trans. C. Casillas and V. Navarro. Valencia: Pre-textos, 1976.

Díaz, Gonzalo. *Historia sentimental de la pintura chilena* [Sentimental History of Chilean Painting]. Santiago: Galería Sur, 1982.

———. *Sueños privados, ritos públicos* [Private Dreams, Public Rites]. Santiago: La Cortina de Humo, 1989.

Dittborn, Eugenio. *De la chilena pintura historia* [On the History of Chilean Painting]. Santiago: Galería Época, 1975.

———. *Mapa: Airmail Paintings = Pinturas Aeropostales*. London: ICA, 1993.

Donoso, Claudia, and Paz Errázuriz. *La manzana de Adán / Adam's Apple*. Foreword by Juan Andrés Piña. Trans. Gonzalo Donoso Yáñez. Santiago: Zona Editorial, 1990.

Dorfman, Ariel. *Death and the Maiden*. New York: Penguin, 1991.

Eltit, Diamela. "Sobre las acciones de arte: Un nuevo espacio crítico" [Concerning Art Actions: A New Critical Space]. *Umbral* 3 (October 1980).

———. *E. Luminata*. Trans. Ronald Christ. Santa Fe, N.M.: Lumen, 1997.

————. El padre mío [Father of Mine]. Santiago: Francisco Zegers Editor, 1989.

————. "Concerning Literary Practice." Trans. Alice A. Nelson. *Mediations* 22 (spring 1999): 136–43.

Escobar, Ticio. "Cultura y transición democrática en Paraguay" [Culture and Democratic Transition in Paraguay]. *Revista de crítica cultural* 3 (1991): 33–35.

Forster, Ricardo. "El encogimiento de las palabras" [The Shrinking of Words]. *Revista de crítica cultural* 2 (November 1990): 33–35.

Galaz, Gaspar. *En Tierra* [On the Ground]. Santiago: Galería Plástica Nueva, 1989.

García Canclini, Néstor. "Los estudios culturales de los 80 a los 90" [Cultural Studies from the Eighties to the Nineties]. *Punto de vista* 40 (September 1991): 41–48.

————. *Hybrid Cultures: Strategies for Entering and Leaving Modernity*. Foreword by Renato Rosaldo. Trans. Christopher L. Chiappari and Silvia L. López. Minneapolis: University of Minnesota Press, 1995.

Garretón, Manuel Antonio. *El proceso chileno* [The Chilean Process]. Santiago: FLACSO, 1983.

————. *Reconstruir la política* [Rebuilding Politics]. Santiago: Editorial Andante, 1987.

————. "Los intelectuales han muerto" [The Intellectuals Have Died]. *Página abierta* 74 (September 1992).

Garretón, Manuel Antonio, Saúl Sosnowski, and Bernardo Subercaseaux, eds. *Cultura, autoritarismo y redemocratización en Chile* [Culture, Authoritarianism, and Redemocratization in Chile]. Santiago: Fondo de Cultura Económica, 1993.

Hopenhayn, Martín. "¿Qué tienen contra los sociólogos?" [What Do You Have against Sociologists?]. In *Arte en Chile desde 1973: Escena de avanzada y sociedad* [Art in Chile since 1973: The Avanzada Scene and Society], 93–99. Santiago: FLACSO Document 46, 1987.

————. *El humanismo crítico como campo de saberes sociales* [Critical Humanism as a Field of Social Knowledge]. Santiago: FLACSO Document 445, 1990.

Huyssen, Andreas. "Mapping the Postmodern." *New German Critique* 33 (fall 1984): 5–52.

Ivelic, Milán. "La transgresión de los límites" [The Transgression of Limits]. In *Cultura, autoritarismo y redemocratización en Chile* [Culture, Authoritarianism, and Redemocratization in Chile], ed. Manuel Antonio Garretón, Saúl Sosnowski, and Bernardo Subercaseaux, 121–33. Santiago: Fondo de Cultura Económica, 1993.

Kay, Ronald. *Del espacio del acá* [From the Space of Here]. Santiago: Visual, 1990.

Lechner, Norbert. "Desmontaje y recomposición" [Dismantling and Recomposition]. In *Arte en Chile desde 1973: Escena de avanzada y sociedad* [Art in Chile since 1973: The Avanzada Scene and Society], 25–31. Santiago: FLACSO Document 46, 1987.

Montecino, Sonia. "Testimonio y mujer: Algunas reflexiones críticas" [Testimonio and Women: Some Critical Reflections]. In *La invención de la memoria* [The Invention of Memory], ed. Jorge Narváez, 119–26. Santiago: Pehuén, 1988.

Morales, Leonidas. "Walter Benjamin y la crítica literaria chilena" [Walter Benjamin and Chilean Literary Criticism]. In *Sobre Walter Benjamin: Vanguardias, historia, estética y literatura (Una visión latinoamericana)* [On Walter Benjamin: The Avant-Garde, History, Aesthetics, and Literature (Latin American Perspectives)], ed. Gabriela Mussuh and Silvia Fehrmann, 215–21. Buenos Aires: Alianza Editorial / Goethe Institute, 1993.

Moreiras, Alberto. "Postdictadura y reforma del pensamiento" [Postdictatorship and Reformed Thought]. *Revista de crítica cultural* 7 (November 1993): 26–35.

Muñoz, Gonzalo. "Una sola línea para siempre" [A Single Line Forever]. In *Desacato: Sobre la obra de Lotty Rosenfeld* [Disrespect: On the Work of Lotty Rosenfeld], 57–68. Santiago: Francisco Zegers Editor, 1986.

———. "Manifiesto por el claroscuro" [Pro-Chiaroscuro Manifesto]. In *Arte en Chile desde 1973: Escena de avanzada y sociedad* [Art in Chile since 1973: The Avanzada Scene and Society], ed. Nelly Richard, 53–56. Santiago: FLACSO Document 46, 1987.

———. "Lo que no nos mata, nos hace más fuertes" [What Doesn't Kill Us Makes Us Stronger]. Paper presented at the seminar "Modernidad/postmodernismo: Un debate en curso" [Modernity/Postmodernism: An Ongoing Debate], Instituto Chileno-Francés de Cultura [Chilean-French Cultural Institute], Santiago, August 1987.

———. "El gesto del otro" [The Other's Gesture]. In *Cirugía plástica* [Plastic Surgery], ed. Thomas Bierbaum, Gunter Blank, and Matthias Reichelt. Berlin: NGBK, 1989.

Olea, Raquel. "Brevísima relación de la literatura actual" [Very Short Account of Literature Today]. In *1990–1994: La cultura chilena en transición* [1990–1994: Chilean Culture in Transition], ed. Ana María Foxley and Eugenio Tironi, 141–43. Santiago: Secretaría de Comunicación y Cultura, 1994.

Oyarzún, Pablo. "Crítica: historia" [Criticism: History]. In *Arte en Chile desde*

1973: Escena de avanzada y sociedad [Art in Chile since 1973: The *Avanzada* Scene and Society], 43–51. Santiago: FLACSO Document 46, 1987.

———. "Arte en Chile de treinta años" [Thirty Years of Art in Chile]. *Official Journal of the Department of Hispanoamerican Studies* (University of Georgia, 1988).

———. "Bleicher Glanz"/"Parpadeo y piedad" [Blinking and Mercy]. In *Cirugía plástica* [Plastic Surgery], ed. Thomas Bierbaum, Gunter Blank, and Matthias Reichelt, 58–60. Berlin: NGBK, 1989.

Pastor Mellado, Justo. *El fantasma de la sequía* [The Phantom of Drought]. Santiago: Francisco Zegers Editor, 1987.

Pérez, Carlos. "Variaciones sobre un cadáver exquisito" [Variations on an Exquisite Corpse]. In *Cadáver exquisito* [Exquisite Corpse]. Santiago: Catálago Ojo de Buey, 1990.

Rama, Angel. "Indagación de la ideología en la poesía" [Inquiry on Ideology in Poetry]. In *Literatura/sociedad* [Literature/Society], ed. Carlos Altamirano and Beatriz Sarlo, 209–56. Buenos Aires: Hachette, 1983.

Richard, Nelly. *Margins and Institutions: Art in Chile since 1973*. Special issue of *Art & Text* (Melbourne) 21 (1987).

Sarlo, Beatriz. "Intellectuals: Escision or Mimesis?" In *The Redemocratization of Argentine Culture, 1983 and Beyond: An International Research Symposium*, ed. David William Foster, trans. Juliette Spence, 49–58. Tempe: Arizona State University Center for Latin American Studies, 1989.

———. "La historia contra el olvido" [History against Forgetting]. *Punto de vista* 89 (December 1989): 11–13.

Skármeta, Antonio. "Todas las libertades, la libertad" [All Freedoms, Freedom]. In *1990–1994: La cultura chilena en transición* [1990–1994: Chilean Culture in Transition], ed. Ana María Foxley and Eugenio Tironi, 95–102. Santiago: Secrectaría de Comunicación y Cultura, 1994.

Subercaseaux, Bernardo. *Sobre cultura popular* [On Popular Culture]. Santiago: CENECA, 1985.

———. "Nueva sensibilidad y horizonte 'post' en Chile" [New Sensibility and the "Post" Horizon in Chile]. *Nuevo texto crítico* 6 (1990): 135–45.

———. "Política y cultura: Desencuentros y aproximaciones" [Politics and Culture: Misencounters and Approximations]. *Nueva sociedad* 116 (December 1991): 138–45.

Tironi, Eugenio. *La Torre de Babel* [The Tower of Babel]. Santiago: Ediciones Sur, 1984.

Valdés, Adriana. "Señales de vida en un campo minado (la situación chilena y la hipótesis de un arte refractario)" [Signs of Life in a Mined Field (The

Chilean Situation and the Hypothesis of a Refractory Art)]. Photocopy. Santiago, 1977.

————. "Gonzalo Díaz: Pintura por entrega"/"Gonzalo Díaz: Painting on Commission." In *Arte contemporáneo desde Chile/Contemporary Art from Chile*, 10–21. New York: Americas Society, 1991.

————. "Gestos de fijación, gestos de desplazamiento" [Gestures of Fixity, Gestures of Displacement]. In *Cultura, autoritarismo y redemocratización en Chile* [Culture, Authoritarianism, and Redemocratization in Chile], ed. Manuel Antonio Garretón, Saúl Sosnowski, and Bernardo Subercaseaux, 135–46. Santiago: Fondo de Cultura Económica, 1993.

Vattimo, Gianni. *El fin de la modernidad* [The End of Modernity]. Barcelona: Gedisa, 1986.

Vidal, Hernán. *Dictadura militar, trauma social e inauguración de la sociología del teatro en Chile* [Military Dictatorship, Social Trauma, and the Inauguration of a Sociology of Theater in Chile]. Minneapolis: Institute for the Study of Ideologies and Literature, 1991.

Yúdice, George. "Testimonio y concientización" [Testimonio and Consciousness Raising]. *Revista de crítica literaria latinoamericana* 36 (1992): 207–27.

Zima, Pierre. "L'ambivalence dialectique: Entre Benjamin et Bakhtin" [Dialectical Ambivalence: Between Benjamin and Bakhtin]. *Revue d'esthétique* 1 (1981): 131–40.

Zurita, Raúl. *Escrituras en el cielo* [Sky Writing]. Printed flier. Santiago, 1982.

————. *Literatura, lenguaje y sociedad (1973–1983)* [Literature, Language, and Society (1973–1983)]. Santiago: CENECA, 1983.

————. "Nace 'la vida nueva'" ["New Life" Is Born]. *Artes y letras* supplement to *El Mercurio* (Santiago), 25 July 1993.

————. "Raúl Zurita y su locura de escribir en el desierto" [Raúl Zurita and His Madness of Writing in the Desert]. *La Época* (Santiago), 13 August 1993.

Index

CENECA (Center for Research on Cultural and Artistic Expression), 56, 109 n.13; and sociology, 59
Centro Imagen (gallery), and CADA, 25
Chilean art. See art, Chilean; avant-garde art
Chilean artists. See specific artists (e.g., Diamela Eltit, Paz Errázuriz)
Chilean voices, expressed in art, 14–15, 41, 92–93
Chilean women writers, voices of, 17
citation; and discourse of the crisis, 53–54; Hopenhayn on, 78; Richard on, 79; Valdés on, 77–78
"Common Grave" (Dittborn), 9
coup, 1973. See 1973 coup
crime scene, photograph as, 9
crisis, poetics of the, 81
critical culture, 87
critical pluralism, and cultural diversity, 72–76
critical practices; and mercantile hypervisibility, 94–101; registers of, 84
critical thought, and the social sciences, 51–63. See also social sciences, Chilean
critics, on "new scene," 44
cultural context, meanings in, 67–68
cultural criticism, 89–94, 98–101
cultural democratization, achieving, 72–73
cultural development, and social integration, 89–94
cultural diversity, and critical pluralism, 72–76

cultural field, unofficial, 56
cultural politics, theorists on, 80–84
cultural practices, 74, 84–89
cultural symbolization, 65–68
cultural works, and reinventing memory, 2–3
culture: after 1973 coup, 41–42; critical, 99–101; and "new scene," 56–57; and politics, 66, 77, 79–80; public scene on, 73; and the left, 40–43
culture, national, schizophrenia of, 94, 96–97
culture of difference, democratic, 76
culture-spectacle, 73–74

Death and the Maiden (Dorfman), 19. See also Dorfman, Ariel
de Certeau, Michel, 104 n.8
deconstruction: art's reaction to, 32; and reconstruction, 39–50; and ruptures in art, 44–47
Deleuze, Gilles, 3, 104 n.4
del Sarto, Ana, 103 n.5
democracy, staging, and politics of difference, 65–76
democratic culture, of difference, 76
democratic transition, years of: and literature, 75; and social sciences, 71. See also 1973 coup; post-coup Chile
democratization, cultural, achieving, 72–73
desert, Chilean, in Zurita's work, 35, 37
destruction; art's reaction to, 32; and reconstruction, 39–50

detained-disappeared, family members of, 9–10
difference; and differentiation, 89–90; politics of, 65–76
Difficult Loves (Calvino), 86
Díaz, Gonzalo, 31, 105 n.14, 105 n.15, 105 n.26, 105 n.39, 105 n.40; "Lonquén 10 años," 18
the discard: aesthetics of, 14–18; art on, 31
discontinuity, and memory, 11–14
discourse of the crisis, 52–54
discourses of order, vs. gestures of resistance, 79–84
Dittborn, Eugenio, 9–10, 31, 83, 105 n.19, 105 n.26
diversity, cultural, and critical pluralism, 72–76
Donoso, Claudia, 16, 105 n.34
Donoso, José, 96
Dorfman, Ariel, 95, 106 n.42, 112 n.#; *Death and the Maiden*, 19; public response to, 2
Duchamp, Marcel, 26
Duvachelle, María Elena, 112 n.#

East (Muñoz), 13
Eltit, Diamela, 17; *Father of mine*, 16; *For the Fatherland*, 13, 104 n.10, 105 n.28, 105 n.33, 105 n.35, 106 n.6, 111 n.29
Errázuriz, Paz, 17, 105 n.34; *Adam's Apple*, 16
escena de avanzada: art in, 46; and critical thought, 52–55; criticism of, 32, 47–48, 62; on the institution of art, 24–30; and power, symbolic, 47–50; practices of, 55–58; and signs, 47–50; and the social sciences, 55–58, 60;

split in, 31; unification of artists by, 44; and works by, 44–46; of writing, 6. *See also* "Oh, South America!" (CADA); "So As Not to Die of Hunger in Art" (CADA)
Escobar, Ticio, 110 n.4, 110 n.5
"Escrituras en el cielo" (Zurita), 29
Este (Muñoz), 13
experience, art as transformation of, 27–28

Father of Mine (Eltit), 16
FLACSO (Latin American Faculty of Social Sciences), 55, 59
Flaubert, Gustave, 86
Forster, Ricardo, 109 n.6
"Fosa Común" (Dittborn), 9
Foucault, Michel, 70

Galaz, Gaspar, 108 n.13, 108 n.14
García Canclini, Néstor, 68, 109 n.27, 110 n.6, 110 n.19, 110 n.33, 110 n.34, 110 n.35
Garretón, Manuel Antonio, 65, 87, 107 n.3, 107 n.4, 110 n.1, 110 n.13
gestures of resistance, vs. discourses of order, 79–84
Gramsci, Antonio, 70
Guattari, Félix, 3, 104 n.4

historical memory, 12–13, 21
history, Chilean: forgetting of, 1–2; reading through Benjamin, 4, 14; retelling of, 59. *See also* social sciences, Chilean
homeless, and identity, in art, 16–17
Hopenhayn, Martín, 56, 104 n.9, 108 n.‡, 108 n.12, 109 n.11, 109 n.29, 110 n.36; on citations,

78; conversation with Bravo, Richard, and Valdés, 77–101; on culture, 79–80, 82, 99–101; on difference and differentiation, 89–90; on memory, 94–95; on schizophrenia of national culture, 94, 96–97; on social sciences, 85

Hoy, and CADA, 25

Huyssen, Andreas, 107 n.22

"I"; in art of "new scene," 47; in photographic portraits, 8

identification photograph (ID), and identity, 8

identity: Benjamin on, 18; crumbling of, 7; and the homeless, in art, 16–17; in photography, 7–8

impurity, of memory, 6. See also memory

institutions; avant-garde on, 33; confines of, overflowing, 24–30

intellectuals, critical; in present-day Chile, 70–71; redefined, 68–72; role of, 77

International Conference on Latin American Women's Literature, 50

Ivelic, Milán, 111 n.28

John Paul II (Pope), 112 n.**

Kay, Ronald, 105 n.17

language, official, 5, 40

Latin America, intellectuals in, 69–70. See also intellectuals, critical

Latin American Faculty of Social Sciences (FLACSO), 55

Lechner, Norbert, 87, 106 n.10, 108 n.27, 109 n.19

the left: after 1973 coup, 42; and culture, 40–43; on the intellectual, 69–70; on "new scene," 47–50; traditional and renewal, 42–43

Leppe, Carlos, 31

Lihn, Enrique, 12

limits, and art, CADA on, 28–30

literature: in democratic transition, 75; in "new scene," 46; as outlet for Chilean voices, 41; and politics, 66

"Lonquén 10 years" (Díaz), 18

loss, and forgetting, of post coup Chile, 1

manifestations, used by traditional left, 43

La manzana de Adán (Errázuriz), 16

Maquieira, Diego, 13

Marxism, critique of, 42–43

masterpieces, "new scene" on, 24

meaning: and Chilean art, 4–5; in cultural context, 67–68; and discourse of the crisis, 53–54

Medina, Hugo, 112 n.#

Mellado, Pastor, 105 n.20

memory: and discontinuity, 11–14; historical, 12–13, 21; Hopenhayn on, 94–95; impurity of, 6; in "Neither grief nor fear," 36–37; and politics, 18–19; and the present, 18–21; reinventing, 1–4; subjectivity of, 19–20; as trace and reinscription, 10

mercantile hypervisibility, and critical strategies, 94–101

militancy, of CADA, 28–30

military coup. See 1973 coup

milk, distribution of, and CADA, 25–26

modernity, Latin American, and Chilean social science, 61–62

Montecino, Sonia, 105 n.32

Morales, Leonidas, 104 n.2, 104 n.3

Morandé, Pedro, 111 n.*

Moreiras, Alberto, 104 n.1

Mosquera, Gerardo, 103 n.7

movement, and culture, Valdés on, 90–91

La muerte y la doncella (Dorfman), 19

Muñoz, Gonzalo, 13, 31, 44, 49, 105 n.36, 107 n.19, 108 n.9, 109 n.17, 109 n.18

Museo Nacional de Bellas Artes (National Fine Arts Museum), and CADA, 27

museums, and CADA, 26–27

narrative, and historical memory, 13

national culture, schizophrenia of, 94, 96–97

National Fine Arts Museum (Museo Nacional de Bellas Artes), and CADA, 27

"Neither grief nor fear" (Zurita), 35–36

neo–avant-garde, 23–37. See also avant-garde art; CADA (Colectivo de Acciones de Arte)

"new scene" (avanzada): art in, 46; and critical thought, 52–55; criticism of, 32, 47–48, 62; on the institution of art, 24–30; and power, symbolic, 47–50; practices of, 55–58; and signs,

47–50; and the social sciences, 55–58, 60; split in, 31; unification of artists by, 44; and works by, 44–46; of writing, 6. See also "Oh, South America!" (CADA); "So As Not to Die of Hunger in Art" (CADA)

news items, detained-disappeared as, in art, 10

1980s, and the social sciences, 60, 62

1973 coup: art and culture after, 41–42; artists' response to, 45; the left, after, 42; as ordering act, 40–41. See also democratic transition, years of; post-coup Chile

"Ni pena ni miedo" (Zurita), 35–36

nueva escena. See "new scene" (avanzada)

official field of discourse, and unofficial field, break between, 39–40

officialism, Bravo on, 92–93

official power, language of, 5, 40

official versions, 90–91

"Oh, South America!" (CADA), 25–26. See also CADA (Colectivo de Acciones de Arte)

Olea, Raquel, 111 n.27

order: call to, and politics, 41; discourses of, vs. gestures of resistance, 79–84; military coup as act of, 40–41; will to, and sociology, 58–59

Oviedo, José, 103 n.7

Oyarzún, Pablo, 7, 34, 104 n.13, 106 n.1, 106 n.2, 106 n.4, 107 n.25,

Richard, Nelly (*continued*)
103 n.6; use of "yes" and "no,"
104 n.‡; works in translation, 103
n.7
Rosenfeld, Lotty, 46, 109 n.12
ruptures, in art, and deconstruction, 44–47

Sarlo, Beatriz, 70, 106 n.41, 110
n.12, 110 n.23
scene, public, on culture, 73
schizophrenia, of national culture,
94, 96–97
Sentimental Education (Flaubert), 86
signs: and "new scene," 47–50;
production of, "new scene" on,
24; and refractory art, 5–6
Skármeta, Antonio, 73, 110 n.20
"Sky Writing" (Zurita), 29
"So as Not to Die of Hunger in Art"
(CADA), 25–27, 30–31. *See also*
CADA (Colectivo de Acciones de
Arte)
social criticism, of "new scene," 32
social integration, and critical
culture, 89–94
Socialist Renewal, 42–43
social sciences, Chilean: and aesthetics, 51–63, 77; and art,
51–52; and cultural practices,
84–89; and Latin American
modernity, 61–62; and "new
scene," 55–58; and order, will
to, 58–59; and retelling of history, 59; and years of democratic
transition, 71
Sosnowski, Saúl, 65, 110 n.1
Subercaseaux, Bernardo, 65, 107
n.24, 108 n.7, 110 n.1, 110 n.18

symbolic power, and "new scene,"
49–50
symbolization, cultural, 65–68
symbols, in work of "new scene,"
44–45
systems of power, and "new
scene," 47–50

testimonio (testimonial), 14–17
theater; and rehistoricizing of
past, 11–12; and subjectivity of
memory, 19–20
La tirana (Maquieira), 13
Tironi, Eugenio, 106 n.13
trace, memory as, 10
traditional left, 42–43, 47–48. *See
also* the left
tribe, notion of, Valdés on, 78–79

United Nations, and CADA, 25
university, in Chile: and Benjamin's
works, 2–3; transformation of,
due to military intervention, 52
unofficial field: of culture, study
of, 56; and official field, break
between, 39–40
"Urinal" (Duchamp), 26

Valdés, Adriana, 4, 104 n.6, 104 n.7,
105 n.14, 105 n.15, 110 n.7, 110
n.8, 110 n.22, 110 n.30; on citations, 77–78; conversation with
Bravo, Hopenhayn, and Richard,
77–101; on culture and politics,
83–84; on Dorfman's play, 95–
96; on movement and culture,
90–91; on notion of tribe, 78–79;
on social sciences, 86–89
Vattimo, Gianni, 106 n.9

NELLY RICHARD is the founder and director of the journal *Revista de crítica cultural*, in Santiago, Chile. She is the author of *La estratificación de los márgenes: Sobre arte, cultura y política/s* (1989); *Masculino/femenino: Prácticas de la diferencia y cultura democrática* (1993); *La insubordinación de los signos: Cambio político, trans-formaciones culturales y poéticas de la crisis* (1994); *Residuos y metáforas: Ensayos de crítica cultural sobre el Chile el la transición* (1998). She edited *Políticas y estéticas de la memoria* (2000), and, with Alberto Moreiras, *Pensar en/la postdictadura* (2001).

ALICE A. NELSON teaches Latin American Cultural Studies and Spanish at the Evergreen State College. She has written extensively on contemporary Chilean culture, most recently, *Political Bodies: Gender, History, and the Struggle for Narrative Power in Recent Chilean Literature* (2002), and has published translations of short works by several Chilean authors, including Pía Barros, Soledad Bianchi, and Diamela Eltit.

SILVIA R. TANDECIARZ teaches Hispanic Studies at the College of William and Mary. A specialist in Southern Cone Cultural Studies, she has published articles on the relationship between Peronism and cultural production, feminist theory, and film. Her translations of theory and poetry have appeared in *South Atlantic Quarterly*, *Revista de crítica cultural*, and *Tameme*, and she published her first book of poetry, *Exorcismos*, in 2000.

Library of Congress Cataloging-in-Publication Data

Richard, Nelly.

[Insubordinación de los signos. English]

The insubordination of signs : political change, cultural transformation, and poetics of the crisis / Nelly Richard ; Alice A. Nelson
and Silvia R. Tandeciarz, translators.

p. cm. — (Post-contemporary interventions) (Latin America in
translation/en traducción/em tradução)

Includes bibliographical references and index.

I S B N 0-8223-3327-9 (cloth : alk. paper) —

I S B N 0-8223-3339-2 (pbk. : alk. paper)

1. Chile—Civilization—20th century. 2. Chile—Politics and
government—1973–1988. 3. Chile—Politics and government
—1988– 4. Politics and culture—Chile. 5. Politics and literature—Chile. 6. Authoritarianism—Psychological aspects.
7. Adjustment (Psychology)—Chile—History—20th century.
I. Title. II. Series. III. Series: Latin America in translation/en
traducción/em tradução

F3100.R5213 2004

983.06′5—dc22   2003019460